Gender, Patriarchy & Sexual Mind Control

Breaking Free

Cate Montana

ISBN 979-8-9911139-0-8

Printed and bound in the USA

Cate Montana
Maui, HAWAI'I
2024

Also by Cate Montana

- *Cracking the Matrix: 14 Keys to Individual & Global Freedom*
- *The E Word: Ego, Enlightenment & Other Essentials*
- *Unearthing Venus: My Search for the Woman Within*
- *Apollo & Me*
- *The Heart of the Matter: A Simple Guide to Discovering Gifts in Strange Wrapping Paper* (With Darren Weissman)
- *Ghetto Physics: Redefining the Game* (co-written with William Arntz)
- *Shamanism In the New Millennium* (compiled and edited)

"If repression has indeed been the fundamental link between power, knowledge, and sexuality since the classical age, it stands to reason that we will not be able to free ourselves from it except at a considerable cost."

Michel Foucault

Contents

Introduction

Google the word "freedom" and check out the images. Most show women and men leaping into the air or standing on mountaintops, arms spread wide, embracing life with exuberant joy. Some show birds soaring and chains breaking against a backdrop of golden sunshine, bright clouds, and flower-filled meadows.

Faces are turned towards a glorious, unexplored horizon. Bodies exude aliveness. Nothing can stop these people. They seem to live in a world with no boring jobs and overdue bills, no hangovers and health issues, no chem trails and lockdowns, no censorship or global elites pressing the "reset" button.

Unfortunately, one trip to Costco or Walmart, dissolves the fantasy. Watching all the stressed, unhappy people in the stores, it's clear that none of us actually live in that world. In the US, about the only place freely exuberant beings seem to dwell is in photoshopped sales and PR images.

I mean, how many people are jumping for joy in your experience? How many people feel free? Unfettered? Fulfilled? Happy even? How about yourself?

Freedom curtailed

Ever since the film *The Matrix* came out in 1999, there has been ongoing speculation (and no small amount of scientific evidence) theorizing that humanity is caught in some kind of artificial matrix not of our own making. Some scientists believe we're living in some kind of computer simulation. Whatever the truth is, you and I are definitely living in a world that's subject to extremely intricate and powerful layers of *programming*—programming that is 180 degrees out of phase with life, liberty, and the pursuit of happiness—programming that seems precisely designed to ensure low self- esteem, anxiety, fear, confusion, depression, poor mental, emotional and physical health, lethargy, acquiescence to authority and indifference to life itself.

Why and how is this happening? And what do gender, patriarchy, and sex have to do with this? And what do we do about it?

That's what this book is all about.

A couple of givens

Before diving into the main topic of sexual mind control, there are two foundational principles that need to be quickly addressed because without some explanation, much of the material in this book will seem strange, if not incomprehensible. These two precepts are:

#1) Human beings are spirits inhabiting physical bodies.

First and foremost, our essential nature is non-physical. As spirit, we are intelligent beings of pure love energy occupying seemingly physical bodies on a seemingly physical planet called Earth. Religious texts across history, cultures, and all nations refer to our innate spiritual nature.

On top of this, the briefest of dives into quantum physics will tell you that *there is nothing actually physical about our bodies or our reality*.

What?

Think about it. Einstein's famous equation, $E=MC^2$ tells us that energy and mass are equivalent. And at the subatomic level there is no such thing as a physical particle. Electrons, positrons, neutrons, muons, quarks etc. are all concentrated packets of energy. There is no teeny, tiny, infinitesimally small grain of some *thing* underpinning our reality—it's energy all the way down.

> Bottomline: Spirit and matter are the same thing, showing up in one of two ways: Formless energy and the *appearance* of form

Why aren't most people aware of this most fundamental of all truths? It's because...

#2) Humanity is being messed with and deceived.

Since time immemorial, there have been elite Powers That Be (and I'm not talking about politicians) that don't have your and my best interests at heart, whose ultimate goal is global domination and control.

To facilitate this agenda (currently referred to as The Great Reset or the New World Order), it serves this corrupt, socio-pathic faction (the hidden puppeteers behind politics and politicians) to make the global population as weak, pliable, and disordered as possible.

To that end, the majority of social structures that have been created on this planet in the last two-thousand years—political structures, economic systems, religions and spiritual organizations, health systems, educational structures, food systems, etc. —have been created in ways specifically designed to keep humanity ignorant, divided, and in scarcity.

The goal is to keep you and me in a state of constant fear, stress, confusion, unhappiness, and lack—a state designed to keep us all on the treadmill of competition and at each others' throats, feeling chronically inadequate, insecure, and totally distracted by all the insane demands on our time and attention.

Taking a look at our world today, wouldn't you say this agenda has been pretty successful so far?

If this seems crazy to you, think about how our health and cognitive functions are being reduced through the rapid poisoning of our water, air, soils, and food supply with chemicals, GMOs, and industrial waste. Since the mid-1970s, Western IQs have been steadily dropping every year. As well, research shows that the typical Western diet has a negative impact on the brain, resulting in cognitive dysfunction and neuro-degeneration.

This is not accidental.

Additionally, increasing pressure for pharmaceutical interventions, incessant mind-numbing violence in media/entertainment/gaming and soul-deadening educational practices—all inhibit our ability to think independently and set ourselves free from propaganda and external control.

Our nation's population is also in a serious state of physical decline. For the last sixty years, Westernized populations have been plagued by an epidemic of "civilization diseases," chronic non-infectious degenerative diseases—obesity, diabetes, cancer, cardiovascular disease, autoimmune diseases, to name just a few. All these diseases were rare a hundred years ago and non-existent in hunter-gatherer societies.

Unseen presence

If it seems ridiculous and paranoid to believe all this is being purposefully done to us, it's a great indicator that: 1) as a decent human being—as a spirit being of love—you find it almost impossible to imagine such evil doings by any other person or group of people; 2) It's also an indicator that your decency is being used against you to keep you brainwashed and blind to the obvious truth that is clear once the blindfold has been removed.

I've written an in-depth book about the overarching control agenda on this planet called *Cracking the Matrix: 14 Keys to Individual & Global Freedom.* It goes waaaay deep down the rabbit hole and involves the exposure of an unseen, interdimensional influence that has been the hidden driver behind the deliberate degeneration of humanity for thousands of years.

Priests and shamans, philosophers and mystics, medicine men and women of every culture on every continent in the world have clearly described this non-physical presence and named it. Swiss psychiatrist Carl Jung equated this deceiving intelligence with the Antichrist. Modern-day philosophers and science fiction writers often refer to these beings as mind parasites. Native Americans call them Windingo and Wetiko. Tibetan Buddhists call these interdimensional interlopers "hungry ghosts." Of course, in Christian literature this presence is reduced to a singular (rather ludicrous) persona named Beelzebub, the devil, or Satan.

I'm not going to talk much about this interdimensional influence in this book because our social programming makes it incredibly difficult for most people to accept the possibility of a negative, non-human presence on this planet as actually "real." Even though this truth has been revealed over and over again in every possible way, from the Bible and the Rig Veda to modern movies, the deceivers are very good at deceiving and keeping their presence hidden.

If this subject resonates and intrigues you, check out *Cracking the Matrix*. If it doesn't intrigue you, no worries. To get value out of this book, it's not necessary to accept that this negative influence exists. Although, I have to say that once you start researching this topic, pretty much all the weirdness about humanity and our history finally makes sense.

But, now, on to the subject at hand.

Sponges

We are spirits of pure love. And if you want proof, all you have to do is spend 30 seconds looking into the impossibly clear eyes of a little baby. *Who We Really Are* shines through loud and clear.

We are spirits of pure love. And if you want proof, all you have to do is spend 30 seconds looking into the impossibly clear eyes of a little baby. *Who We Really Are* shines through loud and clear. (As well, if you do this, you'll also realize what a load of garbage the whole Abrahamic belief in original sin actually is. A more perfect example of the kind of deliberately-degrading, negative programming people have had inflicted upon them for thousands of years cannot be found.)

As well, you'll instantly realize how wide open and impressionable we are when our spirit essences land in a human body.

In this innocent, virginal, pre-intellectual state, we soak up sensory information like a sponge, unconsciously gathering sensory input from the world around us. We receive impressions about our species, ethnicity and gender before we even have the words to fit the knowing. For example, I unconsciously received the message that I'm a human Caucasian female long before I understood what a human being even is!

We unconsciously absorb identities around national origin, beliefs about God and our economic status. We soak up our parents' political orientation and work ethic. Then comes school and we learn that humans supposedly evolved from apes and that we live on a spinning globe in an isolated solar system hurtling through the deep emptiness of space. We learn from his-story that our species is aggressive, greedy, cruel and violent.

Before you know it, we're seeing ourselves as "Syrian" or "Armenian" or "American," "Christian," "Jewish," or "Muslim," and are willing to pick up a gun to prove our national/racial/religious superiority and protect our beliefs and territory from the aggression and possible takeover by "others." And we do this as easily and unconsciously as we learn to walk, climb stairs and run.

Spiritual biology

Of all the unconscious identities we take on, I'm going to go out on a limb and proclaim that our sexual identity is the most powerful. I say this because 1) sex hormones are the most intense and potent biochemicals in the body, 2) the subject matter is emotionally fraught and 3) unlike other identities—political, philosophic, spirito-religious, economic etc.—sexual identity isn't a social construct.

It's *biological.*

And before you freak out over the political incorrectness of that statement, stop for a moment and remember that biology at the subatomic level is actually energy and not truly "physical" at all.

What does that mean? It means that the traditional sexual paradigm where you have only two choices for sexual identity based upon physical genitalia—male and female—is grossly incomplete.

Instead of looking at our bodies from a strictly physiological perspective, believing we're nothing but a bunch of walking/talking meat sacks—conglomerations of cells, hormones, biochemicals, genitalia, and things like that—for accuracy's sake, we also have to talk about biology and sexuality in terms of energy. And if we do that, biology and our sexual identity become tremendously fluid.

If human beings are spirits inhabiting physical bodies and physical matter isn't really physical, *spirit and matter are fundamentally equivalent.* Additionally, from a quantum physics perspective, there are no borders and boundaries between objects. The world—from cars, to steam engines, to human beings, to avocados, to the kitchen table—is made up of fluid interpenetrating fields of energy. Nothing is "fixed" as it were. The world is simply composed of interpenetrating energetic frequencies—frequencies that can be adjusted and changed at will.

This is why it's possible (not common but possible) for some avatars—people who have mastered their energetic body—to walk through walls, levitate, bi-locate and accomplish all sorts of other "magical" feats. (Think Dr. Strange in *The Multiverse of Madness.*) This is also the whole basis for the alchemical understanding that, with the proper esoteric knowledge and skill, lead can be turned into gold.

At this level of human expression, a man or woman who has grasped their spirit nature, understood the energetic nature of the world and their body, and learned to fluidly express however they want to express physically is hardly concerned with gender issues. At this level of consciousness, gender issues and sexual identity become limitations and are irrelevant.

But, if we don't know Who/What We Really Are—if we're stuck believing we're a bunch of evolved apes (because that's what we've been told), or maybe creatures made from clay bumbling around on the global playing field like a bunch of peasants operating at less than ten percent of our actual brain capacity ... if we believe we're just a bunch of competitive meat sacks trying to survive in a dog-eat-dog world—how can we ever step up and into our potential?

If you're an elite Puppet Master with world domination on your mind, people knowing Who/What They Really Are is a nightmare made real and the last thing you want to have happen. Because when people understand Who/What They Really Are, they cannot be manipulated and controlled anymore.

As within, so without

Another thing that makes "biology" so fluid, is the amazing fact that our (apparently) physical bodies match our individual, unique spirits precisely.

It's well known in psychiatric circles that people suffering from Multiple Personality Disorder, now known as Dissociative Identity Disorder in the DSM-5 and Merck Manual, manifest different physical traits according to which persona they're expressing. In some cases, one personality might have allergies while none of the other personas experience them. Or the allergies might be completely different. Or one persona might need glasses to read or manifest color blindness and other personas do not. Sometimes even eye color can change.

Basically, our bodies are designed to resonate to the consciousness of our individual spirit and our spirit's particular intention(s) for any given lifetime. And consciousness is fluid, not fixed. Our bodies and our reality are incredibly plastic and malleable. Our potentials are unknown.

And yet science and society have combined to solidify the view that we're nothing more than dysfunctional stimulus/response machines with no spirit, no life spark ... just chemical processes running amok, "genetic accidents" with no reason or purpose. The image of human being that has been impressed upon us over and over again, is an image of insignificance, weakness, fallibility and corruption.

And we wonder why peoples' spirits are depressed and we feel lost?

Meanwhile, our young people are busy tearing old paradigms apart, desperately seeking a reality that makes sense, trying to find an identity that's outside the box. Good for them! Unfortunately, they're going about it the way they've been unconsciously programmed to do so—by further narrowing and compartmentalizing reality.

By creating more and more labels and boxes to live in.

To date young people have created and labeled over 80 gender roles, from bi, straight, gay, lesbian, trans, and queer, to cisgender, demigender, diadic, gender binary, polygender, intergender, pangender, soft butch, and on and on and on. And there's nothing wrong with this. It's just that it's just more of the same of what we've already got.

The unspoken need of beings who don't know Who They Really Are is: "Give me a label so I can identify myself in a way that makes sense to me. Then maybe I'll be happy and feel sane in this insane world."

But labels will never make us happy. Nor will they ever set us free.

To be free, we have to turn around and see Who/What We Really Are, and start walking in a different direction. We have to understand that there are scary agendas afoot designed to reduce us from brilliant, ecstatic, autonomous spirits having adventures in physical bodies on planet Earth to robotic, tuned-out drones.

To be free, we have to understand the mechanics of how this is being done so we can dodge the traps and pitfalls that have been set up for us. And one of the darkest, most powerful traps that has been set to ensnare us in the matrix is false ideas about sex, sexual identity, and gender.

So, let's get started removing the veils.

Chapter 1

Getting Started

Scientific reductionism has brought humanity to the point of believing that the five senses are all that is available to us. This, of course, leaves out any non-physical realities such as soul, spirit, love, emotions and thought, all of which science has reduced to mere byproducts of neuronal brain function and "molecules of emotion." 1

This purely physiological view of the human being is problematic for us (and ideal for the Puppet Masters) because if I can be convinced that all I am is cellular and chemical functions—if my identity is totally wrapped up in biology and body parts and how I "present" with those body parts—then I will be more willing to accept physical solutions as the only answer to all my problems.

Want to get ahead in the rat race? Work longer and harder and beat the crap out of the other guy. Tired of your mind and body being so slow and weak? Depressed? Take some pills. Low self-esteem? Lose weight. Lonely? Go to a bar. Scary new virus going around? Get a synthetic vaccine. Want to "be all you can be"? AI augmentation can take care of that! Don't you want the global data net in your head, just like in the movies?

Of course, you do!

Never mind neural lace implants can be pulsed with EM frequencies carrying information and instructions from satellites around the globe. The technology already exists. And if you don't know what I'm talking about, try watching the movies *The Signal* (2007) and *Cell* (2016). Or for that matter the first film in *The Divergent* series (2014).

Occult understanding

I know various social institutions have given this word all sorts of weird supernatural and even demonic overtones. But did you know that "occult" simply means "hidden?"

Spiritual knowledge has traditionally been hidden and labeled occult and demonic to keep it out of the hands of the general population. And this is deeply problematic. Because, if only a small number of people in the world have special knowledge about the more hidden aspects of life and the real nature of human beings, while the vast majority of people are operating from a vastly incomplete data set (but don't know it) ... the result is a deeply flawed culture that creates a deeply flawed and grotesquely limited reality for people to live in.

Just like the one we have today.

For the Puppet Masters, power is defined strictly in terms of control: control *over* other people and resources. And because knowledge is power, esoteric knowledge—occult spiritual knowledge beyond the ken of mere physical science—is especially guarded **because it teaches men and women how to deal with the unseen forces that underpin and rule "physical" reality.**

The Powers That Be can't have the masses gaining power

over *them*. So, the Abrahamic religions of Judaism, Islam and Christianity all forbid people from dabbling in the "dark arts"—the occult practices of divination, tarot, numerology, astrology, ritual magic, alchemy, and the Eastern siddhic practices of manipulating matter.

And yet kings and queens, popes and bishops, the ancient blood-line families, the elite, all use occult practices for the simple reason that these things work. But they make damn sure these practices remain mostly in their hands by programming the masses to steer clear of their use by associating them with evil forces and the devil. Sure, a few people are into these things, but the mainstream media makes sure they're always presented as weirdo fortune tellers, Wiccans and whack jobs to ensure the practices remain silly in the eyes of the general public.

I'm not a Bible person. But I do remember this line from my Catholic school days:

> "My people are destroyed for lack of knowledge."[2]

This is a great truth. So, let's get on with addressing this lack with a few fundamental *occult* facts about sex that you need to know.

Electromagnetic polarity

Scientists have calculated that less than .00000000000000000000000000000001 seconds (that's 32 zeroes!) after the Big Bang, electrons and positrons were created—the negative electromagnetic charge and the positive electromagnetic charge. Why is this significant? Because electromagnetic polarity is the foundation of "physical" worlds and human bodies. It's the "stuff" from which they are created.

And electrons and positrons are pure energy.

In the Eastern traditions, electrons—the negative charge—are labeled "yin," while positrons—the energetic positive charge—are labeled "yang." The ancient yin/yang symbol for the positive/negative energetic forces underpinning this planet looks like this:

Now, Eastern esoteric science teaches that the energy of both electrons and positrons and the electromagnetic fields they emanate have physical *qualities and characteristics.* Some of the energetic qualities of the negative electromagnetic charge (yin) include: fluidity, flexibility, inclusiveness, connection, softness, roundness, internality, rest, receptivity, and darkness. Yin is represented by the black portion of the symbol.

Some of the energetic qualities of the positive electromagnetic charge (yang) include: structure, fixedness, hardness, pointedness, externality, action, guardedness, singularity, isolation, and light. It's the white portion of the symbol.

The dot of white in the black section and the dot of black in the white section symbolize the truth that when it comes to "physical" expression, except for electrons and positrons themselves, there is no such thing as "pure yin" or "pure yang." There is always a bit of yang present in the yin and vice versa.

The sperm-like shape of these two polarities shows constant spiral movement between the two forces. As in life, nothing is static and fixed.

Adjectives not nouns

The electromagnetic foundations of the world are a binary construct. But aside from 1) positrons and electrons and other charged particles, and 2) the pure white of unfiltered sunlight and the pure black in the depths of a black hole where no light can exist, I can think of no purely binary expressions to be found in the physical world. No clear-cut absolute opposites.

Yes, there are certain polarized (yet complementary) characteristics that are basic to the three-dimensional reality that electrons and positrons help build. Complementary characteristics like up and down, right/left, slow/fast, dark/light, night/day, in/out, smooth/rough, concave/convex, cold/hot, wet/dry, subtle/obvious, fluid/fixed, open/closed, passive/active ... just to name a few. But in actuality these seeming opposites are not opposite at all because they all exist on a sliding scale of relativity.

Philosophically, religiously and morally we are programmed to think in absolute binary terms. In terms of black and white, right and wrong, and good and evil. But when it comes down to actual living, what happens? It seems that expressing ourselves is a matter of almost infinite shades of grey.

Space isn't "empty" and the scientifically-pursued "Absolute Zero" of space is purely conceptual. Absolute cold doesn't exist. Nor does pure heat. The number of potential points between point A and Point B is infinite, so I can't even use the comparison of finite versus infinite.

There is no absolute up and no absolute down. Right? How far right? If I walk far enough and circle the globe it just brings me back to my left. And if I'm looking in a mirror, right appears to actually be my left. Gender? Modern generations understand that being locked in a binary gender box, forced to play out a fixed, polarized gender role where no such thing actually exists, is horribly wrong.

In truth, all of creation and all the "things" in it—all the planets and creatures populating those planets—are a beautiful *blend* of complementary polarities and yin/yang qualities.

In Eastern thought, positive/yang and negative/yin are like adjectives coloring the world ... electromagnetic influences molding and imbuing matter with qualities that range across an infinite spectrum of potentials and possibilities. So now let's look at some physical examples.

Some examples

A cave is concave and dark—obviously strongly yin. A sword is linear, sharp and pointed— obviously strongly yang. But most things on planet Earth are an obvious blend of both polarities. Take, for example, a rose bush. The petals are soft and rounded and yin. The stems are tough, the thorns pointed, sharp and yang.

The balance and degree to which something is yin or yang can vary and change over time. For example, let's take a mountain. Mountains are essentially yang in nature because taken as a whole, mountains are qualitatively convex, fixed, hard, and rough.

But some mountains are more yang than others. A sharply pointed volcano is qualitatively more yang than a softly-rounded mountain in Appalachia. The volcano is extremely active, pointed, hot, hard, rough, and bright. The worn-down, tree-covered mountain in Appalachia is softer, curved, more fertile, smoother and darkly verdant. However, after a billion years or so, the once highly yang alpine volcano has been worn down by weather and other geologic actions. It slowly becomes more and more yin. It's still a mountain and yang, but it's a more yin expression of yang than it was in its youth.

A willow tree is more yin than a pine tree. Shorter, rounded in overall shape, fluid, with soft flowing leaves, the willow tree is flexible in its early years, easily bending with the wind. Then, as it ages, trunk and limbs become more fixed and inflexible, and thus the tree becomes more yang in its expression. It's still a willow tree and still a yin expression of "tree." But it moves into a more yang kind of yin expression over the years. This changeability is also an expression of its essentially yin (unfixed, fluid) nature.

On the other hand, a pine tree is tall, erect, pointed, with sharp needles that penetrate the sky. Except in the early more pliant (more yin) stages, pine trees aren't flexible or yielding. The expression of a pine tree is much more yang than yin.

Once you "get" the way yin/yang forces work, it's easy seeing what's what in the world around you. New York skyscrapers are extremely yang. Domed mosques in Istanbul are yin with pointed yang spires. Cell towers are yang, rounded dish receivers are yin. Etcetera.

Woman and man

From a yin energetic perspective, let's look at the "physicality" of woman. Soft and round, her reproductive organs are spacious and internal and held in the dark. She receives the sperm of the man who actively penetrates her. As child-bearer she rests in gestation, remaining inclusive, flexible and fluid, out of necessity adapting to changes within her. Enigmatic, internal ... nothing about her is obvious.

Resonating to the yang energetic quality of hardness, men's bodies tend to be angular and tough. Their penises are pointed and external and also get hard. Vibrating to the tune of action and strength, men often take the most direct route they can find from point "A" to point "B." Why? Because they can. They're qualitatively built for it and linear directness is part of the innate yang energetic.

As anybody who has spent much time around the extreme of a highly-yin woman knows, she is more focused on internal issues and can be something of a homebody. As anybody who has spent much time around the extreme of a highly-yang man knows, he can be easily fixed upon an external goal and will often isolate himself out of necessity to accomplish self-imposed tasks.

And if you think this sounds sexist and binary, please remember: I'm describing the *extreme* energetic, qualitative polarities of yin and yang forces as they manifest in male and female bodies. The truth is:

Just like rose bushes and Eastern mosques, everything in the "physical" world—including woman and man—contain both yin qualities and yang qualities.

Generally speaking, women are biologically/energetically more yin/feminine expressions of the hominid species. Shorter, rounded, softer, weaker, passive/receptive, with internal genitalia and hidden wombs. *Generally speaking*, biologically/energetically, men are more yang/masculine expressions of the hominid species. Tall, pointed penis, hard, tough, rough, active, external, obvious genitalia etc.

And in case you're getting triggered by all this binary talk, I'm going to stop for a second and appropriately talk about ...

Social conditioning

As a life-long feminist and an energetically yang woman, I have spent my life breaking through glass ceilings. I was the first female TV production engineer ever hired by ABC Sports back in 1978 when there were almost no female electronics engineers in the industry anywhere in the world. Certainly not at the network level. And none in national sports telecasting. Breaking into that game and beating out all the men was brutal.

Back then—and up until around the year 2000—if I had read words describing women as "softer, weaker, passive and receptive" I would have gone ballistic because, I'd spent my whole life desperately trying not to be any of those things. Why?

Because for two-thousand years and more, energetic feminine (yin) qualities like softness and receptivity had been consistently belittled as pathetically "less than" by men conditioned into a patriarchal mindset. My disgust for all qualities labeled "feminine" (yin) knew no bounds. Rest? Passivity? Emotionality? Softness? Roundness? Frilliness? Images of fat, whiny women dressed in lace, flopping around on chaise lounges eating bonbons all day floated through my head.

My 1960s and '70s social conditioning had clearly taught me that being receptive and passive meant I was being a pussy —somebody who would be walked on by the whole world. Being emotional guaranteed I wouldn't be taken seriously.

Roundness meant I was fat. Softness meant I was weak. I wanted to be smart, tough and aggressive so I could get ahead in life. Yeah, the feminine was associated with great intuitive capacity and that seemed cool. But intuition couldn't hold a candle compared to the importance of logic and intellect.

Perceiving the world through a masculine lens, every qualitative aspect of the feminine seemed undesirable and negative. Hell, the feminine was the negative polarity itself! The left side of the body (the yin side) was labeled "sinister" in Latin. The sins and weakness of Eve had ejected mankind from the Garden of Eden. The darkness of her womb was associated with the evil dark dealings of Satan and the occult.

While the masculine ... ah, the masculine was all things positive, bright, beautiful and desirable.

The light and right of God were masculine. Intelligence, intellect, and logic were the preeminent glories of man. The ability to take and sustain action was all-important. Strength, mastery, and structure ensured safety. Man was synonymous with power and glory. Woman was synonymous with powerlessness, insignificance and sin.

It wasn't difficult choosing which side I wanted to emulate and be on.

But here's the deal. Just like all the driven, stressed-out men around me, I had been brainwashed into condemning and avoiding expressing all the balancing complementary yin energies that would truly liberate me as a human being.

Here's a shocker I'll get into more deeply later: "Patriarchy" has nothing to do with men. It has *everything* to do with the Powers That Be creating deliberate social programming designed to unbalance and mold human beings into controllable drones with no "off" switch—drones that will work themselves to death in the factories and corporations, mines and farms, pursuing safety via competing for money and material goods ... all of which are designed to remain scarce and tough to attain.

Think about the yang energetics: active, aggressive, linear, focused, intellectual. Manipulate the yang half of the human race (*the yang half of both men and women*) into believing these qualities are supreme, then dangle the carrot of material wealth and security in front of peoples' noses and BINGO! You've created active, aggressive, linear, focused, intellectual hamsters who will kill themselves on the hamster wheel—rats who will endlessly run the race, serving as a power source providing endless goods for the elite who own the factories, corporations and resources.

They'll run and run and run without even thinking about it. Because unlike communist countries where nobody is free and everybody knows it, Western nations have been designed to look like they're democratic and "free." And almost nobody sees through the illusion. As the great German writer Johann Wolfgang von Goethe pointed out:

> "The best slave is the one who thinks he is free."

Hidden meanings

Now, let's briefly look at the words describing energetic yin qualities. Being raised in an appallingly skewed, patriarchal mindset, I had no idea what words like "passive" really meant. All I knew was what men thought they meant—men who were as hopelessly brainwashed around the subject as I was.

Recall how people are manipulated into thinking that spiritual knowledge is "occult" and basically the doorway to the Devil's playground so they never look into deep spiritual wisdom and remain powerless? Same thing with yin energetics. Humanity has been relentlessly steered *away* from understanding what the "feminine" nature really is. Because the feminine is the gateway into the subtle realms ... enabling humans to not only access spiritual knowledge, but to *embody* and experience life beyond the appearance of physicality.

Yin/feminine energetics—passivity, rest, internality, receptivity, inclusivity—form the entire foundation of Eastern meditation practices, balancing the yang qualities of action, penetration and external focus. Embracing yin energetics along with the yang allows human beings to be WHOLE human beings, embodying ALL energetic qualities available to us in this universe. Which throws the prison doors wide open.

Without embodying the other half of Who We Really Are, the world will continue to be all ON switch and no OFF switch. All external and no internal. All action and no wisdom. Which is precisely where the whole world is at today, with burned-out, exhausted women and men working their asses off on a raped, depleted planet.

So, if you're getting triggered by some of the words or ideas I'm setting out here—hang on. Breathe. Understand the very fact that you're triggered reveals deep brainwashing that has to be expunged for you to come home to yourself as a whole human being and spirit of love.

Not surprisingly, triggers are now being seen as things to avoid at all costs. But triggers are helpful! They're neon signs pointing towards where we've been manipulated, wounded, and scared. They reveal what needs healing. And how can we take care of ourselves and others and heal unless we know where the wounds are?

Endless variations

Some men are extremely yang like a pine tree. Some men, though biologically male, are more yin like a willow. Some women are highly yin and others (like me) highly yang in their qualitative energetic expression. The possible variations on the spectrum of yin/yang combinations are endless. That's what I meant earlier when I said that looking at biology through the lens of spirit and energy versus physicality gives us an incredibly fluid, unlimited reality.

But the vast majority of the world has gotten deliberately programmed into playing out extreme sexual/physical polarized yin/yang roles. Which is one of the major reasons there is such a powerful and necessary social movement in younger generations against binary sex roles today.

Let me wrap this chapter up with an archetypal example of highly polarized male/female sexual expression. In Tennessee William's play *A Streetcar Named Desire*. the extremely yang main character, Stanley Kowalski, is a brutish New York thug—rough, highly sexed, aggressive, deeply identified with his physical strength and the harsh realities of street life. His classic yin counterpart is the aging Southern belle, Blanche DuBois, a soft, fearful, pliable and vulnerable woman who lives in fantasyland.

William's play points out the violently inevitable electromagnetic attraction of polar opposites—the archetypal attraction of positive and negative forces at play through Stanley and Blanche. Forces that easily overpower every social norm and nicety, ultimately destroying the fragile Blanche.

Although a story of extremes, *A Streetcar* depicts sexual dynamics that, at one level or another, all humans are subject to. Which was Williams' whole point. I mean, why do you think soap operas are so popular? Why do we have millions of songs lamenting the pain, heartbreak, and destructive power of "love?"

But love and sex in themselves are not destructive. What's destructive is our ignorance about love and sexual dynamics.

Stanley and Blanche are oblivious pawns in the global game of mind control. They have no self-knowledge. They don't know Who/What They Really Are. There is no spiritual wisdom showing them a different path and a different way to be. There is no hint of hope in their world. So, they remain prisoners in the matrix.

Can you spell d-y-s-f-u-n-c-t-i-o-n-al?

Dysfunctional, yes. Accidental? No.

EXPLORATION

1) To help disassociate the words "masculine"/yang and "feminine"/yin from the limited idea of gender, take a few minutes and play with the energetic ideas of yang and yin. Look around. What do you see? A desk? A window? Books? A cat? Dog? Sofa? Lamp? Plants? What are the walls made of? How high are the ceilings? What energetic yin/yang qualities do these things embody? What energetic qualities does the room itself have?

Here is a short list of some of the energetic qualities associated with both to work from. Also check out the excellent website: Sacred Lotus Chinese Medicine for a broader understanding.

2) Contemplate the word "occult" and its true meaning, which is "hidden." Have you been frightened by public images and media portrayals of that which has been labeled "occult?"

How is magic portrayed? Specific practices like Tarot and Astrology? Have you been warned against such things? How have these warnings affected you?

Can you see how many of these practices might be useful helping guide you in life? Can you see how if one person has a lot of occult knowledge and uses occult practices that enable them to better understand the more hidden aspects of life processes that they might have an advantage over you and others?

Chapter 2

Subtle Bodies & Sacred Sex

I recently worked with a client I'll call "Carl," who wrote about his journey being born as a little girl named Carlene, eventually transitioning to become a straight man. He was acutely aware of the "wrongness" of his female body by age three. But it wasn't until he began his transition and took his first dose of testosterone at age 29 that, in his own words, "my spirit was able to fully come into my body."

Before he took his first dose of testosterone, he says it was like he "wasn't really here." Then he rubbed the prescribed dose of testosterone on his body for the first time and "within just a few seconds, I was vibrating with a whole new energy—an energy field of maleness that matched my spirit—and, for the first time in my life, my being had something to grab hold of."

I start this chapter with this story because I want to make the spiritual complexity of what it is to be a "human being" more real to you ... real in modern terms we all can relate to. Carl is very clear he was not born in the wrong body. He is very clear he was born biologically female and needed to transition to a male body to become whole. He doesn't identify as male. He understands from the dynamics of his life that his energetic signature is *trans.*

His unique energetic expression is *movement across and between states.* Physically, he now appears as masculine as can be, right down to his full beard and bulging biceps. But a large part of his spirit's expression is highly fluid and yin. His spirit is undaunted by diving into the dark and the hidden places—also a yin capacity. Which is why his spirit could choose this incredibly difficult and terrifyingly painful journey on Earth at this time.

This is major, big time, energetic spiritual alchemy. But is anything like this talked about and understood by doctors, pharmaceutical reps, and trans advocates?

No.

Much of the trans movement is bogged down in its focus on biology and the political issues around trans rights—miring the entire movement in arguments, victimization, and necessary but also monumentally distracting issues like sexual labels, pronouns, and bathroom access. Which is right where the global elites want people to be. Focused on narrow identity issues so that the Big Picture remains invisible.

And, my oh my, is the big picture of Who We Really Are BIG!

Subtle bodies

As a non-physical being, the cumulative information about "you" that determines how you show up in the world is contained in your emotional, mental, spiritual and other bodies. If you or someone you know sees auras, aka the "light body," this is often what they're seeing. Depending on the sensitivity of their "sight," they may well perceive just one or several of these etheric energy layers.

In esoteric understanding, the physical body is the last aspect of the "self" that manifests into what appears as form. There are subtle bodies that precede the physical auric body—among them the mental, emotional, and etheric bodies. It's kind of like a multi-step-down transformer situation.

A graphic representation looks like this:

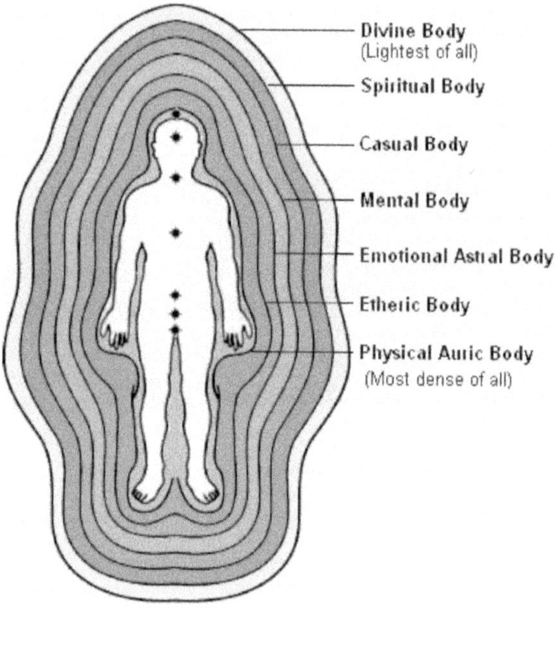

It is your spirit that potentiates and imbues the various non-physical bodies that then determine your ultimate individual physical form, your gender (fixed or fluid), your interests in life and how you roll.

Perhaps your mental body gravitates towards the yin, non-linear side of things and you are born with a deep passion for art and an indifference to intellectual pursuits. Maybe you're highly yin in your physical auric body and are born a cisgender girl, but have a strongly yang mental body and are fascinated with mathematics and logic.

Your lively energy, your slow thoughtfulness, your innate quickness, your capacity for multi- tasking, multidimensional interests, your linearity, your spontaneity, your methodical, plodding approach to life ... all those quirky characteristics, interests, dislikes and likes that make you "you" — all that information that is part of your spirit is stored in your different subtle energy bodies.

Hormones align with all this information and help ground the spirit in the body. Estrogen is yin in nature and augments yin/feminine qualitative expression. Testosterone is yang in nature and augments yang/masculine qualitative expression. Unless there is another spiritual agenda influencing things, sex organs are usually the physical out-picturing aligned with the spirit's energetic signature.

Sacred sex

Nowadays, any references to the "sacredness" of sex are scoffed at. And yet occult wisdom teachings describe the sex act as *divine union*—no matter who and what body parts are conjoining.

Granted, most teachings traditionally depict the Hieros Gamos (The Sacred Marriage) occurring between a man and a woman. But they do so simply because this is the most obvious depiction of the "coming together" of positive and negative electromagnetic forces—the marriage of the complementary opposites of yin and yang/masculine and feminine—from the sexual point of view. It's symbolic.

In truth, the sex of the bodies involved in this joining doesn't matter. All human beings contain both yin and yang energies. Bring the electromagnetic polarities of yin and yang/ feminine and masculine together in coitus via a man with a man, a woman with a woman, or a woman with a man—and the twin sparks of Creation unite, and the physical experience of spiritual oneness can occur via the flesh. If the partners bring conscious awareness to the act, the experience of spiritual oneness can occur.

The Hieros Gamos also symbolizes what is ideally supposed to happen within every individual—the internal unification of yin/yang qualities and full spectrum energetic expression that catapults a human being into wholeness and their full power.

This is the union that brings us back to our true selves. At which point we become the avatar—the master—fully aligned with nature and the whole cosmos.

The power of union

Unfortunately, as the occult understanding of the nature of life and our bodies has been lost in the West, the power of sex and sexual union has also been lost. Sexual union—*consciously* engaged—brings together the thunderous energies of electromagnetic opposites. We're talking physics here. We're also talking about the foundational purpose behind tantric sex, *which is the conscious harnessing and direction of the powers that created the universe.*

At the highest and most sacred level, this deliberate raising and use of sexual energies is directed towards stimulating and opening up the pineal gland in the brain—often referred to as "the third eye." Yang in nature, the pineal is partnered with the pituitary gland, which is yin. By stimulating these two glands with energy derived from the sexual union—especially the powerful quintessential union of complementary opposites via the union of a yang/man and a yin/woman, the psychic centers in the brain are opened and made functional.

Which is the next step on the sacred path to becoming a fully activated, fully actualized human being—aka a spirit of love.

The introduction of sin

Is it possible for two women or two men to consciously engage in sex and use the sexual energies unleashed to drive energy to the psychic centers of their brains? Absolutely! Is it as potent an energy cocktail as the traditional Hieros Gamos? Most likely not. Not because there's anything wrong with the union of same-sex partners. Again, its simply a matter of the natural energies involved that are available to be unleashed and directed.

Either way, harnessing and directing sexual energies for the purpose of "enlightening" the individuals and expanding their capacity for higher consciousness—bringing them closer to knowing Who/What They Really Are—is a sacred act no matter what the sex of the bodies involved,

It's a holy act ... the act of making one whole.

Which, again, is precisely what the global elite do not want the unwashed masses doing. So, how did the Powers That Be manage to keep people from knowing about this and keep them from using sex for the sacred act of becoming whole?

They twisted the idea of sacredness and turned it into an issue of morality.

Priests in all the Abrahamic religions were fed corrupted interpretations of the Hieros Gamos which was only ceremoniously conducted between men and women. They were taught to believe it's "sinful" to engage in sex outside of the sacred bonds of marriage, and that sex between two people who aren't male and female is also morally wrong.

This corrupted teaching has been hammered into people for thousands of years—engendering a legacy of shame, self-hatred, anxiety, and sexual guilt the negative effects of which are epigenetically stamped into the DNA of most Westerners to this day—a debilitating emotional imprint that keeps people confused, depressed and unconsciously convinced that human beings are degenerate slobs that have to be kept in line through moral and legal authority.

Included in this steady diet of religious brainwashing, is the overt message that sex itself is a "down and dirty" activity. It's about fucking, bonking, boning, getting railed, porked and shafted. Getting fucked is a euphemism for being conned and badly used.

The most energetically potent of all human acts has been deliberately debased and degraded into a sordid, furtive humping of strangers in the dark, seeking brief spasms of pleasure.

Why? Well, consider this. If sexual energies are potent enough to stimulate glands in the brain and help wake people up to their true nature, what happens when sexual energies are mixed with shame and guilt? What is getting activated? More shame and guilt—two emotions guaranteed to keep people depressed and asleep. Which brings me around to another sacred use of sexual energies.

Sexual healing

For thousands of years, temple priestesses and priests were trained in specific practices of healing, using the creative energetic forces of sex to provide profound services to humanity.

These highly aware, empathic women and men took others whose minds and bodies had been shattered by war, rape, torture and other abuses and soothed them. They anointed them with healing oils, calmed their spirits, and made love with these tormented souls, returning them to moments of sanity by offering life instead of death, offering pleasure instead of pain.

They tracked the subtle energies of their patients' ravaged energy bodies and understood where to send healing light. They took them into their own sacred bodies—bodies that had not been defiled by war and terror, killing and bitterness—and held these tortured beings in love while they raged and rutted and expressed whatever needed expressing to release the demons inside them.

The bodies of these priestesses and priests were holy ground—temples of love. And yet look at how these sexual physicians are referred to today: *Temple prostitutes.*

What? Why?

You already know the answer—to demean and erase all trace of sacredness and make what these holy women and men did into something else.

Meaningless and trivial

Engaging in sex without an understanding of what's really going on when you "do it," is like putting on a bathing suit, snorkel gear and fins in your living room, thinking you're swimming in the ocean. You can flop around in the gear. You can even have fun doing it. But you're missing the key ingredient—water.

I'm not saying sex has to be some exalted act all the time. You don't even have to know the person you're joining with. *But at the very least understand the actual forces involved and respect them.*

Sexual knowledge is the key ingredient. I mean, come on. Sometimes, when conditions are ripe and a male and female join and the egg is at its most round, fertile and receptive and the sperm is at its most active, pointed and purposeful ... creation itself occurs and new life—a new human—is brought into being.

I don't know about you, but to me, that sounds pretty damned profound. But how is sex portrayed over and over to the masses? Modern magazine articles boast titles like "Forget the morning coffee, have an orgasm to boost productivity."[3] Thus, sex is reduced to a morning routine along with brushing your teeth and flossing—a method of boosting corporate productivity and profits along the way.

This kind of media material is, quite frankly "sinful"—and I mean this in the sense of the original meaning of the word. ("Sin" was an archery term meaning "to miss the mark." Back in biblical days, sin had nothing to do with being a bad person or wrongdoing. It meant you missed what you were aiming for. Try again.)

What I'm trying to say is, it's gross neglect to trivialize sex. It's gross neglect to withhold esoteric/occult knowledge of the forces involved in sex from the general public. Because without the hidden knowledge about the forces being unleashed during sex, people totally miss the mark when it comes to maximizing pleasure, the sense of togetherness and union, and intimacy. And who wants to miss any of that?

Getting beyond programming

Modern generations understand that being locked in a binary gender box, forced to play out a fixed, polarized gender role where no such thing actually exists, is horribly wrong. Unfortunately, this beautiful organic insight by our young people has become a massive "sexual questioning" movement that, while providing options and fluidity, also offers the opportunity for emotional confusion and commercial exploitation.

It's our right and privilege to fluidly express whatever we feel through and with our bodies. But our bodies *already* energetically offer an almost infinite sliding scale of choice and freedom of expression. Gender labels don't free us. The narrow us into boxes with a name tag on them.

I can't help but wonder if the current generation had been been raised to understand the electromagnetic foundation of the world and yin/yang energetics—if they'd been raised outside the patriarchal influences that denigrate all things yin/feminine, if they knew that sex wasn't just "sex" —would the current gender fluid movement even need to exist?

Unfortunately, we haven't been raised with this knowledge. It's been kept hidden because sexual identity is the root essence of our being, and the manipulation of sexual identity and sexual energies has long been one of the primary methods of globalist control.

So, let's take a look at some of the rest of the programming of the past, and expose the lies that have kept us vulnerable, afraid, and not our true selves.

EXPLORATION

Knowing yourself as you do, what kind of energetic yin/yang qualities of your spirit nature have been reflected in your mental body? Your emotional body? Your physical body? In your life choices and occupation? In your home environment? In your sexuality and choice of partners?

What have you been raised to think about sex? How does it compare to the information in this chapter? Can you now begin to see sex in terms of the sacred without bringing religion and morality into the picture?

How has religion and the idea of sinfulness affected your sexuality and sex life? Your family? Friends? Have you felt guilt and shame or embarrassment about your sexuality? If so, how has that affected your life? Your path and your choices?

Chapter 3

The Original Lie

My family wasn't hugely religious. But my mother, wanting to do her Christian duty, dragged me to the local Episcopal church at least once a month on Sundays. There I learned I am an imperfect sinner. (Sinner as in a bad person, not a lousy shot with a bow and arrow.) Along with everybody else in the world, I was the inherently corrupt progeny of Adam and Eve—untrustworthy simply because I was born into a human body.

I struggled against this teaching. The whole idea, delivered in the solemn, hushed atmosphere of church, filled me with disquiet. The sight of all the bowed adult heads around me, calmly accepting the vision of being lowly disgusting worms in the sight of God filled me with dismay. I didn't feel like a lowly worm! I felt alive and vibrant and beautiful inside. Why was I being told such a story?

Unquestioning

Despite my resistance, the constantly repeated image slowly sank inwards, imprinting my psyche and soul. Looking back, I think this teaching was the reason I never questioned the various evil doings in the world around me. The rapes and murders on the nightly news and on TV shows, the starving children in Africa, the conflict, the poverty, the insane prospect of nuclear war. Vietnam.

I didn't question these things because what else could I expect of humanity but misery, mayhem, and madness?

During my teen years, I fantasized that the starship Enterprise would time warp back to the 20th century, and that somehow Mr. Spock and I would meet. In every dream scenario he would ask me to accompany him back to the ship, and I would be invited to go where "no man has gone before."

Reaching my twenties and adulthood, having made no such escape, I dropped the childhood fantasy and turned to the mundane task of growing up and making a living. In other words, I lost myself in another fantasy—that of being a material girl, chasing money, success, sex, drugs, rock n' roll, fast cars, nice houses, and swimming pools. And when career, money, marriage, mortgages and children did not inspire and fulfill, I discovered spirituality and the time-honored path of self-improvement.

I spent the next 20 years trying to be anything but me. A human being. On Earth. Here. Now.

It never once occurred to me that the foundational teaching that humanity—myself included—is sinful and rotten to the core was an intentional lie. I mean, I learned this lesson in the most holy, most trustworthy environment on the planet—*in church.* Why would I ever question the teaching?

Nobody bothered to tell me to look into the pellucid eyes of a baby and see if I found evil there. If they had, I would have cottoned onto the bullshit much earlier.

The concept of original sin

So where did the ridiculous idea of inherent evil in man originate? Although it had been kicked around for a hundred years beforehand, the concept was firmly introduced into Catholic creed by Augustine of Hippo, now known as St. Augustine. (354-430 AD) Despite the fact that his mother was a devout Christian, Augustine spent much of his early life as a sex addict and a drunk until he was introduced to the religious philosophy known as Manichaeism.

Manichaeism, as set forth by the Babylonian prophet Mani (216 AD), outlines the struggle between a good, spiritual world of light (the masculine/yang) and an evil material world of darkness (the feminine/yin) where every person is born into sin merely by the fact of being physical.

And yes, this is the root teaching responsible for the fall of the goddess religions, the foundation of patriarchy, and the subsequent judgment and subjugation of women. Mani arrived at this view because he was coached into it by what he called his "other self"—an invisible "spirit" that talked to him.

The guilt-ridden young Augustine adopted Manichaeism and was "saved," and he assumed the message about the corruption of the flesh was delivered to Mani by a heavenly angel. Of course, Mani never said it was. He said he didn't know where the message came from. He just "heard" it.

In hindsight, 1800 years later, it's easy to see the likelihood of the single most emotionally damaging idea ever to be introduced to humanity being given to Mani by any angel is just about nil. But Augustine used this purported "heavenly message" as a way to explain his own debauched doings as a youth. Converting to Christianity, eventually he became a brilliant theologian, going on to officially ground the idea of original sin into Catholic theology.

And the rest is his-story.

So, where did this message really come from? Well, now would be a good time to embrace the possibility of the existence of a non-physical intelligence that does not have humanity's best interests at heart—an interdimensional presence that has been negatively influencing humanity for a very long time. Doing so goes a long way towards answering questions like this, as well as explaining the machinations of the global elite—the human Powers That Be I keep referring to who are in alignment with these entities and, quite frankly, possessed by them.

But if you find that hard to swallow, no worries. Wherever this lie about human nature came from, the damage has been done, and the real focus needs to be on correcting that damage.

For if you yell at a kid long enough, telling him/her from birth that they are no good, that they are evil and sinful and corrupt ... how is it possible for a child to become much of anything? How could they possibly accept the truth that they are beings of love and light? How could they avoid adopting a terrible burden of guilt, anger and shame about themselves? How could they dodge destructive emotions that would guarantee dysfunction, addiction, acting out, depression—you name it—throughout the course of their lives?

Sins of the fathers

Science is now proving that strong emotions such as guilt and shame are passed down epigenetically from generation to generation—something Systemic Work and Constellations expert Judy Wilkins-Smith calls inherited Emotional DNA.

Our human genetic code creates proteins affecting gene

expression. Epigenetic changes triggered by emotional trauma accompanying stressful events don't alter the proteins produced or alter our genetic code. However, they do create "markers" that are responsible for turning certain genes "on" and "off," affecting how our bodies *read* and then expresses a DNA sequence.

Which means if you had Puritan ancestors that came to America on the Mayflower (like me), to a greater or lesser degree, you're likely dealing with the same deep-seated emotions (and judgments) around sex and the human body that your uptight ancestors experienced. This is what is meant by the biblical expression about the "sins of the fathers and mothers" being passed down to us. It's a reference to the genetically-based emotional heritage that shadows us all at every turn.

Living in the 21st century, over a hundred generations of women and men coming before us have been programmed into the painful teachings of original sin and the pure no-goodness of human nature. And psychiatrists and social workers wonder why modern generations of young people wrestle with low self-esteem? Why they are cutting themselves? Turning to drugs and alcohol, porn and video games to escape themselves and the crazed world that is still being created around them? A world that reflects nothing of the goodness of Who They Really Are?

There is an ancient esoteric teaching that says, "As within, so without." Which means, "As you believe, so you think, act and create in the world." It is not hard to see the effects of this wretched lie on our world, for we have taken this foul inheritance and built from it a world in which politics, government, economics, philosophy, religion, spirituality, science, health, education, entertainment, all reflect the lie.

It's enough to send even the most balanced person straight over the edge.

Ubiquitous message

Even if you were raised atheist and have never heard of original sin, it's hard to escape the negative programming on this planet. One of my many wake-up calls recently was seeing that the relentless, fundamental message of society, religion, and spirituality is basically all the same:

You are not good enough as you are.

I had to be thinner, richer, prettier, smarter, more successful, more competitive, more spiritual, more pure, more enlightened, tougher, kinder, more loving etc. There was an endless list of things I had to do and become in order to be acceptable in this world. Wherever I turned, whether it was TV shows or magazine articles, Sunday sermons or self-improvement workshops, there was always the message that I needed to do something, get somewhere, and be something I wasn't.

Never once did I see a message that said, "You're okay kid." All I saw and heard was basically "You're not okay." And almost every TV show and practically every movie I saw solidified this impression by portraying characters trapped in endless dysfunction, addiction, mindless sex, selfishness, violence, corruption, and greed.

Believing the picture the entertainment industry and legacy media paint of humanity, you'd think murders and rapes happen on every street corner on the planet every 15 minutes. And yet, to this day, I've never once seen a car explode, witnessed a car chase, or seen a murder, robbery, or some gruesome attack happen. Unbelievable. Right?

I've traveled from England through Europe into Russia and Turkey. I've spent months in the Amazon jungles of Peru and Ecuador in South America, lived for years in Central America and briefly in South Africa and India. And the people in all the places I lived were decent and kind.

Everywhere in the world—even in LA, London and New York—everybody I've ever met pretty much wants the same thing: To be left alone to do what makes them happy, find a mate, raise their kids to be healthy and happy, contribute to their community as much as they can and feel fulfilled by living a loving, productive life.

Sure, there are assholes you meet along the way. And I'm not saying there aren't criminals and horrifyingly bad and cruel people in the world. I'm not saying there aren't evil people doing inconceivably awful things to others. Obviously, there are or I wouldn't be writing this. But it's shocking how disproportionate the impact these "bad apples" have in the world. It only takes one power-mad sociopath to influence and destroy the lives, livelihoods and ecosystems of entire nations.

Which is, I think, a testimony to the genuine goodness of humanity as a whole.

And yet we're programmed not to see the goodness that's all around us. Instead, we're programmed to constantly imagine bad stuff which keeps us in fear and destroys our opinions about human beings and, by extension, ourselves.

Talk about a vision guaranteed to obliterate self-esteem, trigger anxiety disorders and keep me running on the treadmill!

A new vision

Albert Einstein is credited with the following marvelous quote: "We cannot solve our problems with the same level of thinking that created them." And he's right. It's time to let it all go. It's time to see beyond the programmed matrix. It's time to finally recognize Who/What We Really Are: Spirits temporarily trapped in an illusion. Beings whose soul purpose is expressing the foundational frequency of existence—pure love—in whatever ways align with our true nature.

It's time to dust off our wings and fly.

EXPLORATION

1) How has the concept of original sin affected you and your life? Did you buy into it? How has it affected the people around you? Your family? Friends? Your culture?

2) Ever feel like you just don't measure up? That there are so many things you have to be, do and say to be cool? To be liked? To be accepted by others? Ever feel you're not enough? That you'll never be enough no matter how hard you study or work or how much money you make or how cool your clothes are or how hot the car you drive is?

Yes, well. That's the program. You're supposed to feel this way about yourself. It makes you more manipulatable. It steers you towards very specific things to think, eat, wear and buy. I remember the first time I really *saw* the covers of women's magazines and what they were selling: Sex, beauty (so somebody will want to have sex with you), weight loss (so somebody will want to have sex with you), and chocolate cheesecake recipes. (The way to a man's heart is through his stomach. And after he's eaten then he'll have sex with you. And if he doesn't want to have sex with you, at least there's the booby prize of chocolate cheesecake to eat.)

The mixed message of sex, weight loss and fattening desserts was shocking when I actually thought about it. No wonder women can never get "it" right. We're not supposed to. But by golly we're supposed to drive ourselves crazy trying!

3) A lot of the crap we feel isn't even *our* crap. We think it is but, as discussed, there are epigenetic influences happening. And then, as spirit beings made of energy, please understand

how we're easily influenced by other energies around us. Ever been in a great mood and then you go to the store or a party and suddenly your mood plummets? It's weird, right?

No, it's not weird. It's just that you picked up the vibes of some other person(s) around you. And all the while you thought it was *you.*

If you're interested in being able to actually manage this situation and not walk around like a psychic sponge, soaking up other energies and influences all day long, here's a quick exercise you can do.

GROUNDING AND CLEARING PROCESS

This is a part of a self-healing modality practice available through Sustainable Love and SOUL ALCHEMY ™ developed by Robin and Joseph Duda. (www.sustainablelove.com)

This process is the beginning step to clearing one's energy field and opening one's awareness to healing energy—a capacity that we all have available as part of our authentic nature and design.

When we are polarized in one element of our being we get out of balance. When we are subject to and processing others' projections and/or are living from our social conditioning, it is more difficult to feel our own genuine nature and inner healer.

In this practice we are focusing on reclaiming and uniting both the action and natural power that run through us, activating the inner healer by energizing the multidimensional Rainbow Frequency which holds: 1) the love from Source, 2) the pure love of Earth, 3) the intelligence of the body and soul's wholeness.

This process enables us to:

- Embody masculine, feminine, and child energies.

- Embody information of other intelligent lifeforms we have experienced in the past.
- Increase our capacity to embody love as our resource for self and other.
- Reconnect to and mobilize our energy body, which serves our desires for wholeness and personal fulfillment, all the while creating the world of our dreams.

PROCESS

You can start off either laying down or sitting.

- Connect with your breath and observe how you are breathing. Don't change anything. Just notice.
- Tune into your body sensations, opening up to an awareness of your inner landscape. (How you feel inwardly ... feelings, sensations)
- Take a few minutes to track your sensations and deeply connect to your body.
- Place your attention on your heart center and focus on anything you are grateful for. This will help your heart open and allow you to sense that opening through loving sensations.
- Take 10 deep breaths while holding each gratitude thought, and sigh as you exhale.

Receiving energy from Source and Soul
Stand up.

- Reach your arms above your head about shoulder width apart.
- From the awareness of your heart, feel the fullness of your chest and say out loud:

"From the power of One Love that I am, I invoke my multi-dimensional rainbow light and Source in my body. I welcome all that I am ready to receive and integrate to come home in present time."

- Repeat as many times as needed until you feel energy building.
- Move your body any way that opens and releases tension. Shake, jiggle, jump, circle your arms ... whatever is spontaneous and energizing.
- Do this as long as you feel connected to the above words. This builds up your energy body.
- Ground the energy with foot stomping or small jumps up and down.

Anchoring into the Earth

Send this built-up Source/Soul energy down into the Earth as if you are growing tree roots.

As you focus on sending energy down into Earth, become aware of Earth as a living being receiving your vibration.

Receiving the Magnetic/Electric current of love from Earth

Speak the following with clarity and strength:

"I honor all elements and creatures of Earth. Thank

you! Thank you for your beauty, harmony and love! My body is one with nature and Earth."

- Take time to repeat this honoring step until you feel your heart open in appreciation for your connection.
- Open your being more to receiving and speak out loud:

"I call forth the power of love from the New Earth. I call forth the rainbow current of Earth and of my wholeness and my nature. I claim my right to my Sovereign Self. Love is my greatest power."

- Scoop up/lift energy from the earth into your field and body, bringing it up through your feet, all the way up into the base of your spine and into your heart. Feel the life/love energy of Earth fill your nervous system. Feel it fill you up all the way to the crown of your head.
- Let any sound that wants to come out with the breath as you continue to repeat the phrases as needed until you feel the power rising.
- Let your body move if and as it wants to.
- Repeat as many times as you feel moved to do so while directing your awareness inward as you speak.

Your voice is your will choosing and claiming your heart's desire. You may be able to feel energy moving up and down inside your body as it opens to more vitality

. . .

Claiming Sovereignty, Releasing and Clearing

Now, say out loud:

"I claim my right for sovereignty on this Earth. I claim my right for male, female, and child union. I claim my right to repair all separation among the inner parts of my being. I claim my wholeness."

At this point your body may sway or slow down in movement as you continue to initiate your own balancing and healing process. As the current of your Source and Earth is turned on, as active and receptive energies and the electromagnetic field are turned on, you now have more power to shed any unloving patterns and energies that have taken up residence inside.

Nature and the Love Source in us know how to heal and harmonize. All we have to do is get out of the way.

Say out loud:

"I release all projections and thought forms from family, religious controls, work, lovers, friends, clients, (etc.) that are in my field or body."

- With your breath and movement, push out anything that is intruding into you energetically.
- Make sounds if you can. (This helps activate and release old suppression energies.)

When you feel clearer, next say:

"I release all mind control from media, technology, educational systems, political systems (etc.) that are suppressing my own thoughts and inspirations."

- With your breath and movement, push these energies out through the top of your head and shoulders. Clap your hands around your body while you keep moving.

When you feel clearer, say aloud:

- "I bless myself free of all anti-life and anti-love energies that are not mine, that are attached to my denied fear, limited beliefs, and/or suppressed emotions."

You may feel called to move or sound more vigorously as you speak these phrases out loud. Take as long as you need to move and repeat.

You will feel a natural calming when your system has moved enough energy.

If you wish to keep moving out inauthentic energies, you can add these other releases.

"I bless myself free of anyone else's emotions that I have taken on and I send them back to their own source."

"I release all unseen forces from known and unknown origins wishing me harm. I release everything that is not loving for me and send them back to their own Source."

The more energy and vitality you put into the words and movements, the more clearing usually results. After you feel more open and clear, acknowledge, again, what you are grateful for.

Personal insights and inner knowing of your truer desires usually follow this clearing process.

After this opening of your inner healer, you may also feel more in touch with emotions that have been suppressed or hidden. The movement of anger and/or fear when you are releasing any "not-love" influences is a positive!

All of us unconsciously absorb negative energies. It's just part of life. But we don't want to hold onto them! Please allow and be grateful for any emotions that move through you. Let go of judging anything that is leaving or people that show up that are tied to your process. If we get caught in blaming ourselves and others, this will just lock in more suffering.

Clearing your field is about attaining freedom and compassion for the journey.

Afterwards

- Integrate your experience by choosing silence for at least 10 minutes. (Longer is fine!)
- Feel free to sit outside or in a safe place where you can go deep and feel and rest in your heart connection.
- Take your time and feel the love. Bask in feeling connected to life and aligned with the Life Force that is you.
- Whatever comes into your awareness, allow it to be there.
- When you feel complete, give thanks to Earth and your Multidimensional Self and feel the Love and your own Soul's essence filling you up.
- Journal and/or share insights with another if it feels right to you.

This process can be repeated everyday to increase health, balance, awareness, love, and all forms of empowerment. Celebrate as you feel your full potential as masculine active and receptive feminine energies of wholeness flower, and more of your own self love allows you to open and heal.

Chapter 4

Love & Purity – Not What We Think

Cosmologists and physicists have discovered a holographic connection between gravity in a three-dimensional universe and, linking it to the quantum nature of the universe's two-dimensional boundary, have theorized the universe is actually a holographic projection.

Yeah, that's pretty dense and confusing. But the idea of the universe as a hologram has actually been around for a long time. And it sure aligns with what physicists have discovered about the energetic, connected nature of reality.

Now, we all know what a hologram is and how it's formed. You take a powerfully coherent light source, such as a laser, and split it into two beams. One beam is bounced off an object that then becomes the information source—let's say an apple. The original reference beam is bounced off a mirror. The beam that bounces off the apple "carries" the informational image of the apple. When the reference beam bounced off the mirror is recombined with the information-carrying beam, a three-dimensional holographic projection of the apple is then created.

But there's a peculiar characteristic specific to holograms that gives us tremendous insight into the extraordinary nature of the universe and the nature of human nature, and that's the fact that one pixel taken from the projected image of the apple contains the whole 3-D image.

A hologram is, therefore, an excellent representation of the ancient esoteric teaching about the oneness of creation. In a hologram, there is the *appearance* of discrete physical objects in space/time—apples and oranges, motor bikes and mountains and people—but the whole of creation is contained in everything that exists, right down to the teensiest microbe. Holograms reflect that.

Which means everything in the universe is not just connected via the quantum field underlying "matter." Ultimately it means everything is one thing.

Native American shamans have described this truth by saying things like: "What you do to nature, you do to yourself." The Sufi mystic poet Rumi explained it this way: "You are not a drop in the ocean. You are the ocean in a drop."

Pretty grand image, isn't it?

A quick aside

But before we get deeper into the actual nature of Who/What We Really Are, I'd like to reiterate how profoundly you and I and everyone else on this planet have been duped into believing all sorts of wrong things about our nature, our history, reality—you name it. And I'd like to do it by telling a story about a dear friend of mine from England.

Alan's family lineage is closely linked to the British royal family, and historically his ancestors were heavily involved in royal doings. He is extremely smart, and when he was preparing to take his Oxbridge exams to get into university to study history, his very wealthy family hired a tutor.

But this "tutor" started off his studies in a very peculiar way.

"From now on you will forget everything you've been taught," the man said. "You will forget everything you've been taught because everything you've been taught up until now is *parrot feed for the masses*. Essentially, none of it is true. Especially not the history you're so fond of.

"You are being groomed, and this is your first step. From now on, you accept nothing at face value. If you want to know something you dig for it—and not in normal bibliographies and research sources. Use your family's contacts as your main resource—they will have the information and records you need. And learn to think for yourself.

"That is what I am here to teach you."

My friend said at that point he became mentally and emotionally paralyzed. (He was only 16 at the time.) His family had hired a man to tell him nothing he'd been taught at all his (very expensive) elite boarding schools was true, that the whole world had been hoodwinked, and that it was up to him to figure his own path through what had suddenly become a very strange and sinister reality indeed.

He stayed traumatized for about six months and then he made a choice—and it wasn't to be "groomed." He broke from family tradition, didn't go to university and went his own way. Which is how I met him living in the US many years later.

More than anything else, Alan's experience gave me confidence as I began to stretch my mind beyond the "normal" stories of what's what. His bloodline has been part of the global elite controlling this planet for almost a thousand years. Knowing someone that close to the actual power center, hearing from him that almost everything presented by educational systems and media is deliberately fabricated propaganda designed to *groom us* to be complacent drones—made it a lot easier to pursue "out of the box" ideas.

I know this is second-hand information. But if you're feeling a little shaky reading all this, perhaps his story might help you as well.

Nature is our nature

So—back to the point. If Source Intelligence (aka God) is all that is (the hologram), and if Source Intelligence (aka God) is "pure love," then everything in existence (the hologram), including us, is made of pure love.

In the Hindu religion, God/Brahman, is formless and transcendent. And yet, at the same time, the world is considered to be a *manifestation* of Brahman—in other words, "the body of God." They are one—but not exactly the same. This situation is (sort of) talked about in Christianity, where humans are referred to as the "children of God." We are one—but not exactly the same.

I never could figure out why there was all this focus on sin in church, when in the very next breath priests would talk about God and refer to us as being His children. I was like, "Wait a minute. If God is love and we're children of God, doesn't that mean we're love too?" But then I'd get the story about trees and apples and snakes, and Adam and Eve being bad and getting kicked out of Eden. Which was just about the craziest story I ever heard. If I'd laid a whopper of a tale like that on my parents, I'd have been sent to my room without any supper.

I never did get a believable answer to my question. And as a little kid, I couldn't sort out why the priests were presenting two conflicting images of humans: children of God/love and children filled with evil. In total confusion, I just let it slide.

It wasn't until I ran across Eastern mystic teachings and quantum physics and discovered the concepts of universal oneness and holographic unification that a realistic understanding of "human nature" clicked for me. If Source Intelligence/God is one (omnipresent) and Source Intelligence/God is pure love ... then everything, at its core, is pure love.

Including us.

Coming home

It wasn't until I ran across a woman by the name of Jacqueline Hobbs, aka Oracle Girl that the phrase "beings of pure love" entered my vocabulary. This is how she refers to people, and there was a *feeling* to the words when I first heard them. A frequency. A *signal* I innately aligned with—kind of like a tuning fork going off when its own home note is struck nearby.

Just saying the words—*I am a being of pure love*—I felt a powerful rightness and a sense of relief. Truth had finally arrived and I knew it.

But for most people in the world, saying these words is a struggle at best. And believing them is almost impossible. If the goal of the Powers That Be is to convince spirits of pure love (children of the divine) that they are sinful, plodding creatures with feet of clay that only deserve to serve and obey a higher authority, then one of the logical first steps after replacing their divinity with sinfulness is to confuse them about the nature of love.

Not only do we have thousands of years of programming telling us the words *I am a being of pure love* are not true, we have layer upon layer of weird associations around the words "love" and "pure." Weird associations and definitions that, as a friend of mine puts it, give us the "perfect wrong understanding" of both.

So, without further ado, let's examine what "pure love" really means.

Confusion

A million sermons talk about love as sacrifice. The suffering and death of Jesus is elevated far above his love and example of the eternal life of spirit. Popular songs croon about how love hurts. How we are betrayed by love. How we are the victims and fools of love. A billion ads and songs and magazine articles try to convince us that sex is love. Soap operas and TV shows depict love as manipulation or the reason people do crazy bad things, like murder their wives and husbands when they're unfaithful or disappoint in some way.

In the world of religion and spirituality, the program of mandatory "goodness" and "positivity" has trivialized love to the point where it means you have to be sweet and nice and "loving" all the time to everybody—even when you don't want to be.

And thus, love becomes hypocrisy.

Science has weighed in and told us love is just a particular biochemical—a molecule triggering cascade reactions felt throughout the body that give us "feel good" feelings that we interpret as love. Oxytocin—the "love" hormone—can be sold and bought as a supplement at the local drugstore.

The God of love in the Bible commands the slaughter of infants because they are born of His enemies, and whole nations of people because they won't bow down to Him.

No wonder we're confused about love!

Love

So, what really is love? Well—if God is love, then love is ... God. And life is the garment of love. The Supreme Eternal Unknowable Infinite Intelligence manifest as a trillion trillion galaxies, supporting growth and ever more life. It is breath and wind, volcanos and fire, the icy chill of snow, a babies' cries and lovers' sighs, aardvarks and zebras, oceans and mud puddles. It is fierce as wild fire and sweet as ripe plums, pliable as clay and rigid as titanium, sensitive, incorruptible.

Love can only be itself, the intelligence and the power sustaining life, death, and everything in between with its own incomprehensible laws supporting the ongoing health and growth of all existence.

> **Love is the life force itself, the power that creates universes and just as impartially grinds them to dust. Love is the eternal flame. The endless enigma. All things known and unknown—more powerful and explosive than a billion suns. This is our nature. This is What We Really Are.**

Purity

Purity is a quality that's hard to describe. Pure water—with nothing else mixed in. Pure white—untouched by other colors. Pure tone—a note with no other notes mixed in. To be pure is to be one thing unmixed, untouched by anything else. Esoterically speaking, purity has always been about retaining the original essence of something.

The occult meaning of "virginal" means *unmixed, integrous with self*. Which is why, when you Google the words "purity" and "virgin," images of pristine water droplets and new-fallen snow crop up. Purity is a powerful singularity—a state so potent it can be instantly felt and recognized as such by a blind man.

Information exchange

From an energetic perspective, when two people of any gender come together in sexual embrace, there is automatically a blending of energies, a crossing of boundaries, an interpenetration of essences. "Swapping spit" swaps more than saliva. It swaps energetic information as well.

What kind of information?

The information of self. Your being and everything that makes you you: Your thoughts, your actions, your emotions, your beliefs, hopes, dreams, fears, history, genetic lineage. Every good and bad thing you've ever thought and done. The whole ballgame. That's what gets invisibly shared.

This is why there's a whole teaching in Eastern Vedic literature warning about having multiple sex partners. Not for any moral reasons. Morality has ZERO to do with this. Rather, it has everything to do with the intermingling of vital energetic information transferred into oneself from too many sources.

Take a glass of milk and add one drop of water and it is no longer pure milk. The same thing with sex. It's an energy dynamic of two people coming together and mixing/blending information along with bodily fluids.

I remember the Indian guru Sadhguru Jaggi Vasudev talking about "ramunabunda" which refers to the condition where a highly sexually active man or woman who takes multiple sex partners can get so mixed up energetically with other peoples' frequency signatures that it can create tremendous psychological confusion and negative emotional turmoil.[5]

I mean, think about it. Have sex with ten people or a

hundred and you're unconsciously absorbing every single one of those peoples' fears, addictions, their traumas from rape, abuse, and neglect, the energetic residues from drugs they've taken, etc. According to Native American shamans, it takes a woman seven years of celibacy before all the energies and programs that got deposited within her along with the sperm from all the men she's been with are released from her body. Men receive the energies and programs as well and have to deal with them. But apparently they aren't as deeply affected as women because they don't receive as much physical "input," so to speak.

When I first learned about this energetic exchange between lovers, I was horrified. I don't know about you, but I've got enough of my own stuff to deal with. I don't need a bunch of other peoples' baggage. Even modern studies show that people having a higher number of sex partners tend to struggle more than others with emotional issues and alcohol and drug abuse.

Obviously, discrimination and selectivity when choosing a sexual partner are advisable.

More warped understanding

Now you know where the whole religious emphasis on virginity and purity comes from. But instead of explaining the actual smart reasons behind not having sex with a lot of people, etc., Abrahamic religions made it about morality and being "good" and not going to hell.

Sure, the other reason behind insisting on women being virginal and pure was to ensure the patrimony of any children coming along. But still. The whole issue of purity has gotten so warped by weird religious teachings and ghastly "ethnic purity" pogroms, that people think of "purity" as something old-fashioned and tyrannical. The very word has been polluted, bringing up negative associations of being uptight, prudish, and neo-Nazi. Either that or innocent to the point of naiveté

And who wants that?

This is the kind of deliberate BS programming that's got to be identified and let go. This is the kind of propaganda that guarantees when people read statements like "You are a being of pure love" they dismiss it out of hand as nonsense. *Everything they've ever been taught tells them it isn't so.*

They have no knowledge about the spirit nature of the human being. They have zero understanding about energy and quantum information. They have ridiculous, poisoned ideas about what love and purity mean.

How can people so programmed ever accept the truth of Who They Really Are?

One last point

Who is "purely me?" Who is that person? What do I really stand for? Left unmolested and unprogrammed, what do I think? Believe? Know? Emanate? Represent?

A large part of the trouble in our world today is we have been taught to look outside of ourselves for the answers to these questions. "Taylor Swift says ... Joe Biden says ... Donald Trump says ... my peers say ... my Rabbi, my mother, my father, my teachers say ..."

We jump on the latest fashion bandwagon, the latest TikTok craze, the latest viral video and parrot the information because it sounds interesting or cool, and maybe it kind of aligns with our values. Maybe. But where did we pick up our values? *From outside sources.* Parents, teachers, priests, politicians, pop stars, and actors. From peers who picked it up from outside sources—parents, teachers, priests, politicians, pop stars, and actors.

Who is "purely me?" Who is that person? What do I really stand for and know? What does a being of pure love look like? Act like? Say? Not say? Choose? Not choose? And what do we mean by the word love? Is it romance and moonlight? Valentines and candy? Heartbreak and betrayal? Getting' it on?

Of course not! But unless we question the mainstream narrative, it's easy to just stay on the surface, accepting the media images and messages we're given. And yet, each and every one of us searches for authentic expression and meaning. Despite what we are told, no human being can be satisfied believing all they are capable of expressing and being is a faceless drone, a robotic cog in a demented, all-consuming, materialistic machine.

You are a being of pure love. And this is something the truth of which you can only feel out for yourself. *Feeling* the essence—the energy of Who You Really Are ... *being* that feeling, that pure signal and following it with no interference from outside sources.

It's quite a lot to take in, I know. But until we know and express Who We Really Are, we're stuck playing who we really aren't. And that, as I'm sure you know by now, is a dreadfully painful place to be.

EXPLORATION

Try it on. Say it: "I am a being of pure love."

A million words might flood your brain, screaming out in denial, telling you it's not possible. That this is stupid. That you're a crappy person. Selfish. Foolish. Unattractive. Not very smart. Not very successful. Blah blah blah ...

Say it: "I am a being of pure love."

Close your eyes and *feel* it ... if just for a moment. It's Who

You Really Are no matter what anybody else outside you says to the contrary.

2) How does it feel? Can you describe it? And if you can't, no worries. The sense of it is so far removed from our normal experiences that it's super difficult to put words to—even for a writer like me!

3) What are your thoughts about love now? Can you see what a crippled (and dysfunctional) mainstream model we've been handed up to now?

Chapter 5

Waking Up Is Gnarly

Remember the scene in the movie *The Matrix* when Neo is unplugged from the simulation? He grips the sides of his slimy glass cocoon, staring in shock and disbelief at the nightmare vision of billions of cocooned people serving the machines as battery sources of power.

Stripped of all illusion about the life he believed he'd formerly been living on Earth, the rude awakening has him puking onto the cold metal floor of the Nebuchadnezzar, the fictional hovercraft captained by Morpheus, as he battles accepting the truth.

Finally seeing the matrix of lies I've spent my whole life enmeshed within has indeed been a reckoning. Maybe not quite so dramatic as Neo's awakening. But having one's illusions stripped away is difficult all the same.

To see that my government doesn't have my best interests at heart. To see that healthcare systems are no longer about health or care but about money, profit, and market share. To see that education has become about programming. To see the bloated monster the corporate entity has become—more powerful than whole nations, driven by the greed agenda of the One Percent focused upon perpetual profit no matter the cost—this is not the vision of the world I ever wanted to see.

It's not what any of us have wanted to see. But in our hearts, in our guts, most of us sense the truth of how deep in fantasyland we've been living. It's why I'm writing this book and why you're here reading it.

As Morpheus puts it to Neo before he takes the red pill: "You're here because you know something. What you know you can't explain, but you feel it. You've felt it your entire life ... that there's something wrong with the world. You don't know what it is, but it's there, like a splinter in your mind, driving you mad."

For sure, it's more comfortable cruising on the blue pill in this world. But eventually the world becomes a dream of madness and we have to wake up.

Layer upon layer

Neo had to deal with two worlds, the world inside and the world outside the matrix. Both were equally real when Neo was in them. But his training outside the matrix was clear. His mission was to manipulate the matrix itself, and thus master the illusory world while still in it.

For us, the situation isn't nearly so clear. We might be dealing with only the one world where our (apparently) physical bodies reside. But our minds are captured and enmeshed in hundreds, *thousands*, of stories—layer upon layer of invisible, interlaced informational matrices that dictate our thoughts and beliefs, choices and actions.

The matrix of religion, hierarchy, superiority, better than and less than; the matrix of politics, power, enslavement and control; the matrix of money, lack and abundance; the matrix of education and intellectual knowledge, linear thinking, science and "facts;" the matrix of guilt and emotional blackmail; the matrices of electromagnetic frequencies and technology, psyops and psychic interference. The matrices of sexuality and gender, guilt and pleasure; the matrices of philosophy and psychology; the matrices of good and evil, materiality versus spirituality; the matrices of fear and all that causes it.

The media matrix—muffling and entombing truth in an endless thread of lies, distortion, propaganda and deception. And then there's the matrix of AI—the greatest and all-too-present threat of all.

The web of stories, the layers of deceit, the depth of the charade, the subtlety of the manipulation on so many levels is breathtaking. No wonder humans are screwed up and confused. No wonder we haven't a clue Who We Really Are. We're like the poignant 1969 ballad songstress Joni Mitchell sang on her *Clouds* album:

"I've looked at life from both sides now
From win and lose and still somehow
It's life's illusions I recall
I really don't know life at all."

Breakthrough

Let me tell you the story that set me on the path to taking the red pill and waking up.

Back in 1999, I was working as the NW editor of the national Native American newspaper *Indian Country Today*. I conducted an interview with John Perkins, founder of the Dream Change Coalition and author of the book *Confessions of an Economic Hitman*. We got to talking about gender issues, and he recounted the following story about an Amazonian shaman sent by the Schuar tribe to live in the United States in order to better understand the Western mindset. The shaman's name was Ipupiara.

"He'd been in the US for about six months, when I got an urgent call from him one day."

"John," said Ipupiara. "Where are your women?"

"What do you mean, 'Where are your women?'" I replied, puzzled. "They're right here, working as bankers and teachers and doctors, raising their children and living their lives. Why do you ask?"

"Well, as you know, the men and women in my tribe have highly gender-specific roles based upon the natural inclinations of male and female," Ipupiara said. "The men hunt. They fish. They cut wood for fires and cut down trees to build huts and canoes. The women cook, make clothes, gather wild edibles and care for the children. As elders, men and women have equal say on tribal council and guide the people together. But there is one job that only the women can perform—a job that is the most important job in the tribe. In fact, the survival of the tribe depends upon this one task."

Intrigued, I asked what that task was.

"My friend, you must know that man is extremely linear and focused. Left to our own devices, we will hunt until there are no more animals in the forest. We will fish until there are no more fish in the rivers, and cut down trees until there are no more trees. It is our nature. Just so, the nature of woman is fluid, sensitive, and receptive. Women are in tune with life—sensing the healthy balance within their family, the larger family of the tribe, and the tribe's balance within the natural world.

"The most important job of my tribe is the women

tell the men when to STOP." He paused, then continued. "John, it is obvious to me and my people that your so-called modern world is headed over a cliff. Where are the women of your nation? Why are they not telling the men to stop?"

A rude awakening

Perkins' story was a one-two punch to my gut. I remember sitting in my office chair, listening to his story, staring out the window, realizing in one split-second that I had no idea how to STOP any more than any of the men in my world did. All my life I'd been running in the "ON" position—a driven woman thinking and acting and working like a guy, relentlessly pursuing "success." Tough talking, hard drinking, overly sexual.

Hearing that story, I realized I had absolutely no idea what a woman really was or what possibilities and powerful mysteries my feminine nature offered.

The story changed my life, setting me on a decades-long quest to discover what the words "masculine" and "feminine" actually mean, deprogramming myself from the patriarchal mindset, while doing my best to understand and embody more feminine attributes and values without trashing the masculine way of being I had learned so well ... or trashing men.

Which was easier said than done. I spent a lot of years being bitter about male domination and patriarchy. I had no idea that some twenty years later I would stumble onto the realization that the sexual programming I'd been subject to was deliberate, and that sexual programming of both women and men was a tool of subjugation and control.

And what a shock to realize patriarchy itself is an artificial construct that has nothing to do with men (aside from abusing the masculine principle) and everything to do with the globalist agenda to enthrall and enslave both men and women ... along with a lot of other mechanisms.

Getting down to it

Waking up to the various ways humanity has been abused, coerced, and programmed to be the *least* we can be in life involves talking about a lot of disparate topics. So far, we've looked at the Eastern view of positive/yang/masculine and negative/yin/feminine electromagnetic charges and their energetic qualities. We've examined how these energetic qualities translate into characteristics like intuition (yin) versus intellect (yang), right brain versus left brain function, emotion versus stoicism, peacefulness versus aggression, spontaneity versus planning, etc.

We've touched on how men and women fully expressing both yin and yang, feminine and masculine qualities in relative balance, can become whole, healthy, integrated human beings capable of experiencing an almost infinite variety of energetic expressions. (All those 80+ modern gender labels and then some!) We've also gotten some philosophical/religious programming out of the way as well.

Now, it's time to look at some other corrosive sexual creations. Like the Battle of the Sexes. But before we do ...

EXPLORATION

If you haven't seen it in awhile, and even if you have, watch *The Matrix,* the first movie in the Matrix series. This book will give it a totally different (more real) context. And if you've never watched it ... wow. You're in for a treat—or at least a lot of food for thought.

Chapter 6

Battle of the Sexes

Whether in the bedroom or the boardroom, the image of the sexes doing fierce, relentless battle is an iconic one. The war has been going on for so long, no one even thinks to question it. Men and women competing and despising each other at some level is "normal." Right?

I don't think so.

Go back to energy for a moment. Go back to the electromagnetic polarities and positive and negative charges. Do they naturally repel each other? Or attract? Look at the yin/yang symbol. Does it look like a cat fight? Or something fluid, dynamic, and harmonious?

Yin/feminine and yang/masculine are energetic complementary pairs. They align and dance with each other congruently, creatively, congenially. If it weren't such a cliché, you could say they complete each other. Which is actually, energetically, what they are designed to do. The yin/yang symbol represents divine oneness.

Yes, in the Land of Appearances where everything seems physical, duality and separation into electromagnetic polarity exists. But the action of EM fields is always towards union, integrity, and balance. Everywhere you look in nature, the yin/feminine and yang/masculine forces work together, blend together, work together, dance together, create life together.

Doesn't it strike you as rather odd, that in all of creation, human males and females are the only organic complementary pair in which the partners are pitted against each other in a wretched battle for domination and control?

The split

When did it start? No one knows for certain. But I suspect it had something to do with the paradigm shift from hunter-gatherer to farmer status. Either that or aliens landed and brought with them the agricultural, land ownership model—which, indeed, is the story engraved in stone and told by many early cultures from Sumer to South America to Indonesia and the rest of the world.

Whatever it was, it took something exceedingly powerful to remove man and woman from the natural order of things and place them in opposition to one another.

The most commonly accepted explanation for the Battle of the Sexes is that the move to a fixed agrarian as opposed to a migratory lifestyle eventually introduced the concept of ownership and commerce. Writing, mathematics, and record keeping —all left-brain yang functions—were introduced to keep things organized. (Structure being another yang quality.)

From there it was a short hop to the concept of inheritance. And from there, an even shorter hop to the need to guarantee paternity so that the land you busted your butt cultivating year-in, year- out, passed to your own progeny and not the local blacksmith's. DNA test kits not having been invented yet, marriage and monogamy (at least for women) was the most expedient answer. From there it was apparently a slow (or rapid) slide towards the ownership of women, iron chastity belts, locked rooms in impregnable castle towers and harems, where they were essentially kept barefoot, illiterate, pregnant, and constantly sexually available to their overlord husbands.

Thus began the reign of patriarchy.

Opponents

And thus began the Battle of the Sexes. Because hey, who wouldn't be pissed off being reduced from a sovereign human being to not even a second-class citizen? What human being—what unlimited spirit being of pure love—wouldn't be filled with rage over being seen and treated as a soulless creature that had been created by God solely for the pleasure and use of man? (And yes, you can be a being of pure love and still express rage. Love is LIFE and contains every expression in existence with no judgement. Rage is an appropriate reaction to being made a slave. Who wouldn't fight over something like that?)

And fight women did, and in the only ways left open to them. Subterfuge. Manipulation. Emotional blackmail. Sexual control mechanisms. Magic. Duplicity and plots. All actions which, if you go back and check out some of the yin energetics —passivity, subtlety, fluidity, darkness, intuition, interior processes—"coincidentally" match and utilize the innate yin qualities of expression.

So, here's the deal. Under normal circumstances—*under life-oriented circumstances*—the internal "occult" processes of the feminine/yin would not be duplicitous, and women would not have gained the unpleasant reputation they have for guile and manipulation. They would, instead, be using their yin gifts constructively.

Under normal circumstances—*under life-oriented circumstances*—the external "active and overt" processes of the yang/masculine would not be brutal and coercive, and men would not have gained the unpleasant reputation they have for tyranny and brutishness. They would, instead, be using their yang gifts constructively.

Under life-oriented circumstances, instead of being pitted against each other, men and women, with their seemingly opposite but actually complementary sets of qualities, would be working together, making things happen in a harmonious, even pleasant and exciting fashion. For example, the Schuar tribe in the Brazilian Amazon that the shaman Ipupiara talked about in Chapter Five.

A movie example

I remember a poignant movie scene clearly depicting men and women balanced in yin and yang expressions working together as a team. I don't recall the name of the film. And, unfortunately, the scene itself centered around a battle. But what played out, although simple, was so telling the image has stuck with me for years.

> A woman in a long gown stands at the slit window in a castle, gazing out across the rolling plains. Behind her, the king and his generals stand around a map table in the middle of the room, heatedly discussing battle plans.
>
> Suddenly, the woman stiffens. Her gaze is internal, abstract, focused. After about 15 seconds, she comes

back to herself, turns to the men and quietly, with infinite certitude, says, "Now. Move now."

Instantly, the king and his men stop what they're doing. *They know she knows.* They've been waiting for her signal. They hasten from the room to set their battle plans into action.

The woman exemplifies what the pure yin does best—internal listening, internal sight into dark hidden places, sensing/feeling information from multiple sources, seen and unseen, and expressing it. The men exemplified what the pure yang does best—planning and taking action. In this simple scene, the two complementary energetics are effectively and potently dancing as one.

But humanity is not operating under life-oriented circumstances, and this whole externally balanced yin/yang life design has somehow been turned on its head. Did this happen naturally? Of course not.

How can something unnatural happen naturally?

A difficult point

With so much of humanity's focus and energies placed upon and occupied with the Battle of the Sexes, what has gone completely unnoticed is the cataclysmic social paradigm shift away from equality, cooperation, and harmony with the natural world that it signals.

Behind the sexual battle lies a pyramidal governmental system where an elite group of humans—royalty and wealthy merchants—suddenly dominate everything and everyone. The elite stand atop the heap, exemplifying and encouraging fierce competition instead of cooperation. The system they implement creates scarcity instead of plenty. Harmony and balance evaporate. Conflict and wars are constant. Suddenly there is confusion and pain, disease, famine, judgment, and isolation. Everyone is pitted against everybody else in a battle for simple survival.

Never before in the history of our world has such an artificial social system existed.

Patriarchy, the subjugation of women, and the Battle of the Sexes, are tools and side effects of an even more all-encompassing overthrow, namely the introduction of an artificial, anti-life social structure that has diminished the quality of life on this planet for millennia, turning the natural order of things upside down.

This societal creation is not an accident. And it's not happening because humans are terrible creatures. We have swallowed a bespoke program of lies designed to make us feel like crap about ourselves and thus more easily fall prey to insecurity, self-judgment and self-hatred; a program designed to lead us into self-destructive thinking and forms of self-abuse like addiction and self-harm; a program designed to drive us into various debased actions, like the harm of others, war, and a general devaluation of all that life has built and evolved through the generations, distorting everything.

Sexual harmony

Genuine balance and harmony between men and women will only arrive when three things happen: 1) We understand the true nature of masculine and feminine energies; 2) we learn to *equally value* the qualities of both yin and yang expressions, and 3) we "get" that human evolution means every individual is free to fluidly express *both* yin and yang energetics and move into energetic/spiritual wholeness.

Yes, the balance of yin/yang energetics in each person will vary. They will even vary over the course of their lifetime. (Remember mountains and willow trees.) That's not the point. The point is:

Equality happens when we value both yin and yang expressions equally.

Sooner or later equilibrium will reestablish itself. What that will look like, I don't know. What I do know is that before solid evolutionary steps can occur, we have to take the blindfolds off and know what we're actually dealing with.

The whole point of this book is exposing the truth about Who We Really Are and all the ways sex and gender have been manipulated and distorted to support the overarching agenda of divide and conquer. The good news is that nature abhors imbalance. Life knows nothing other than life and growth ... so life and more growth are inevitable. And people are waking up!

I envision a time in the not-so-distant future, where people —once again knowledgeable of the hidden forces of creation and the nature of Who They Really Are, savvy about the existence and agendas of corrupt forces and no longer subject to their control—work amicably together, no matter what their sex, ethnicity, religion, age, education, nationality etc.

I think that time is swiftly coming.

So, yay! But in the meantime, let's look at some of the other artificially-created sexual programming designed to keep us from this brighter tomorrow.

EXPLORATION

Equality is not about sameness. It's not about women "suiting up" and imitating men. Or men imitating women. It's about recognizing the importance and equal value of ALL energetic qualities and every individual being able to fluidly express those qualities in whatever balance and combination comes naturally to them.

Mainstream programming is about creating conflict. But please remember that the seeming "opposites" of yin and yang are *complementary*. It's like Jerry Maguire (Tom Cruise) looking at Dorothy Boyd (Renée Zellweger) at the end of the movie *Jerry Maguire* when he says, "You complete me."

Let's look at the yin/yang symbol one more time. Knowing what you now know, having read this far, does the Battle of the Sexes make any sense to you anymore?

Chapter 7

The Erasure of Woman

What is known as the fall of the goddess and the goddess religions was actually the eradication of knowledge about the balance of nature and the erasure of the value and importance of the hidden (occult) aspects of the human being: IE. the yin/feminine side of our humanity.

It's a testimony to the thoroughness of my own patriarchal indoctrination that in 20 years spent seeking enlightenment—a pursuit based upon meditation, stillness and inward-focused reflection, a restful receptivity of mind, and a fluidity of consciousness—I never once saw that what I was aggressively trying to attain in my busy, masculine way, was my own feminine nature.

I was completely blind to the fact that the feminine—which at its energetic essence is pure, open, receptive being—was the gateway to the divine I was so actively seeking. It wasn't until I started writing my first book, Unearthing Venus: My Search for the Woman Within and started to reassess words like "passive" and "receptive," that I realized the patriarchal definitions of such words and the awful bias behind those definitions. At that point, the scales fell from my eyes, and I realized how completely I'd been brainwashed into a one-sided view of life and humanity.

No wonder my world was headed over a cliff—just like the shaman Ipupiara had pointed out. We saw the world like the Cyclops—through the one eye of intellect and reason. "Right" was a matter of might. Money and power were all that mattered. Love and compassion, gentleness and understanding got you nailed to a cross and crucified. We were galloping down a one-way street focused on power, possessions, profit, action, attaining, consuming, and building—ALL attributes of the yang side of nature.

But the fall of the goddess and all that meant was just the first deliberate step in the journey. There was more manipulation to come.

Second step: Turn women into pseudo men

If mankind is to perpetually keep the ON switch ON, the coal fires burning, and the money and profits pouring in, woman—the very embodiment of the yin/feminine—has to be erased from existence. She has to be scrubbed from the human picture lest she stand up and say "STOP!" flip the OFF switch and ruin the game by demanding peace, connection, and respect for life.

The yin qualities women *tend* to embody more easily than men, such as gentle nurturing, patience and an appreciation for the sacredness of life itself, have to be deleted lest they restore balance and sanity to the world. Any softening, any compassion, any slowing down would wreck the techno-progress train hurtling down the tracks, driving us towards a world no one wants except the Powers That Be.

By the start of the 20th century, the first phase of feminine erasure was complete. The first step, turning women into worthless chattel, had been accomplished. Three thousand years of patriarchal rule had all but eliminated any sense of credibility for yin/feminine qualities and values. Now, the second phase of feminine eradication needed to be implemented: Turning women into pseudo men.

Castrated feminism

There is much good to be said about the Feminist Movement. One of the hallmarks of the life force itself is balance, and for women, stepping into the embodied expression of more yang/masculine qualities was a great and much-needed evolution towards internal yin/yang balance and inner harmony.

On a societal level, the original intention of the Feminist Movement was equality and the restoration of women to greater power in the world instead of leaving power solely in the hands of men. **Unfortunately, the Feminist Movement and the way it sought to redress the balance of power between the sexes occurred solely in *masculine terms*.**

In the 20th century, patriarchal dominance was so deeply established that women were unable to boldly step into feminine power. Instead, women had to take power the only way it was on offer: By adopting man's definition of power and taking on masculine power roles in the marketplace.

"Manning up" was the sole option available and man up we did.

Through aggressiveness and fierce competition, women shattered the glass ceilings. We adopted cut-throat attitudes, learning to turn a blind eye to suffering, pollution and resource depletion while serving our shareholders' investment portfolios. We won the right to go into combat to fight and die with the men in wars designed to line the pockets of the elites while supporting their globalist agendas of enslavement and tyranny.

Power-brokering females in power suits conquered the C suites. Sexy, leather-clad super heroines in pushup bras wielded swords and clubs, knives and machine guns, gutting, dominating and fucking men and other women alike. Dull-eyed teens and twenty-somethings trolled for one-night stands in bars just like the guys.

And by necessity and ignorance we called this equality.

Third step: Annihilation

There are two ways to go about achieving balance. One way—the old way we've outgrown as a species—is for polar opposites to balance on the *outside*, the guys doing "guy things" being all tough, manly and warlike, while the women do the softer, nurturing, domestic routine.

This separated, exterior balancing act between the sexes reached its peak in the 1950s with the archetypal, emotionally cauterized, gun-totin' John Wayne strutting along with a stiff upper lip as he served up justice in the world. Meanwhile, the archetypal Marilyn Monroe sex kitten, all dewy-eyed, soft and curvy, brainless and helpless, made dinner in the background.

Two externally balanced yin/yang extremes.

The other option is *internal* balance, which is what humanity is struggling to achieve now. And we're struggling precisely because there is no public awareness of the esoteric dynamics involved in personal and species-wide evolution. Hell, nowadays kids are even being programmed to think there is no such thing as evolution.

We're relentlessly being forced to focus on externals—on body parts—thinking that's the only thing that defines us. With women rushing to the masculine side of the boat to join the guys, to maintain balance, the only recourse has been for the men to start to embody more feminine characteristics.

Definitely a healthy move for the men!

When I see a couple dudes out walking, one pushing a carriage and the other with a baby strapped to his chest, my heart warms. The sweetness of the scene does much to mitigate the damage the millions of images and stories portraying men as mere brutes have inflicted.

It's a beautiful thing seeing men's hearts open, their hands tenderly cradling a newborn or assisting a handicapped person rather than clutching a bloody sword. It's a beautiful thing seeing men being emotionally vulnerable. Seeing them protest for peace and women's rights and a healthy stewardship of the earth.

But ... there is a globalist agenda that doesn't want balance. That doesn't want evolved, integrated, informed women and men standing up for one another and the planet. Which brings me to step number three: Eliminating the feminine nature altogether. And possibly woman herself.

Women have always been sexualized. But today they're not only being sexualized, they're being *copied.* Men are being portrayed as being able to be women—even to the point of birthing and nursing a baby. Sexual identification is focused mostly on the physical, as if breasts and internal sex organs, pouty lips, swaying hips, lace, pretty dresses and eye shadow define the feminine.

Changing the very definition of the word "woman" to "birthing person" is being legally considered. Beautiful AI sex robots are in development. Uterine replicators, a technology that once belonged to the realm of science fiction, aren't far behind.

If woman continues to be consigned to pseudo manhood. If she continues to be reduced to a physical sex and reproductive object, once the AI sex kittens and uterine replicators are rolled out ... of what use is she? If men can become stereotypical "females," who needs women? If the qualities and values that actually define the feminine/yin nature in both women and men remain hidden and are destroyed, where is there hope for tenderness? Sacredness?

If the qualities and values that actually define the feminine/yin nature in both women and men remain hidden and are destroyed, where is there hope for tenderness? Sacredness? Mama bear guardianship and stewardship of the earth?

Where and how will we see that mirrored? How will our children learn these tender values? With the mystery of life itself reduced to body parts and technological machinations, how can mankind be led back from the brink of self-destruction? How will the ON switch ever be switched off?

We have been told forever that "love" is the answer. But the very definition and qualities of "love" have also been degraded. Love is now associated with superficial sweetness, romance and sexuality. It's also been successfully linked to weakness and sacrifice.

That's not the kind of "love" that we need.

We need love that's fiercely aligned with LIFE itself. A potent love that encompasses growth, connection, compassion, grace, beauty and all the other feminine qualities of life. A love that expresses action, determination, focus, grit, fierce protection and all the other masculine qualities of life. *We need the fullness and awesome power of feminine/masculine integration.* Only then will we individually have the wholeness that will enable each of us to stand up and shout, "YES!" to wellbeing and peace and "NO! STOP!" to the wanton greed and destruction, separation and violence that is the hallmark of interdimensional forces and the Powers That Be.

Men and women are extraordinary, powerful spirits of pure love.

It's time to understand and embody what that sentence really means. When we do, then we can create the world we have so yearned to see and inhabit for so long.

EXPLORATION

I know it's a huge statement to say there is a plot afoot to eliminate the yin side of life—and thus, by default, cisgender women who express yin characteristics like empathy, compassion, intuition, inclusion, nurturing and connection—but that seems to be what is happening.

Men flaunting every possible cliché about females, dressing up as frilly, silly, vapid temptresses in heavy makeup and pushup bras is just about the most insulting thing imaginable to both women and men.

Men already contain yin energies and have the capacity to express the yin characteristics within themselves. The feminine element already resides within them. But they'll never be able to express it if they get sidetracked in portraying ghastly patriarchal stereotypes of women.

It's a distraction—a ploy to keep men from recognizing and embodying the power of yin energies/qualities.

Frankly, I'm not sure what "practice" is appropriate here aside from deeply contemplating these energies and bravely examining the sexual dynamics in play in the media nowadays and seeing through the programming.

Chapter 8

Dehumanizing Men

Growing up during the Age of Feminism, I was educated to think and act like a guy. (Do you get the topsy-turvy bizarreness of that one sentence?) Intellectual, logical, aggressive, stoic, end-goal focused, success oriented, highly sexed etc. etc., that was me. But, most of these supposedly archetypal "male" expressions actually have little to do with being a man.

Like women over the last several thousand years, men have been deliberately polarized to one end of the spectrum into a highly unbalanced expression of yang energies that have been distorted to present in various socialized ways.

Neutral yang energetic qualities such as action, linearity, structure and pointedness have been forced into the socialized shapes of intellect, logic, aggression, obsessive drive, success—all grotesque manipulations of the yang/masculine principle applied to biological males (and for the last 70 years females), resulting in a self-destructive, globally-destructive society.

The artificial socialization process of taking yang expression to a distorted extreme while burying all hints of yin, brutally warping both men and women, has the end goal of turning beings of pure love (you and me) into something else altogether.

And the "something else" ain't pretty.

So, what was the process? What was the plan? How do you take a yang-expressing spirit and turn that pure being into a monster?

Separate masculine & feminine principles

To dehumanize men, first, and of utmost importance, comes the creation of a divorce between the energetic qualities and values inherent in the masculine/yang principle from those inherent in the feminine/yin principle.

Once separated into individual opposing camps, masculine and feminine qualities and values can be manipulated and twisted until we have what we experience today: A deadened, rapacious, patriarchal society that has no soul, no joy, no love, no compassion, and no respect for life ... with no end in sight.

Trained violence

We have untold generations of relentless social programming glorifying war, teaching violence, saturating humans in images of death and dismemberment from cradle to grave. War is just a fact of life on this planet, with two World Wars and hundreds of localized, territorial wars, started within the last hundred years alone.

Since the 1950s, we've added non-stop violent visual and interactive "entertainment" (aka propaganda) to the mix. Out of 3,000 studies on TV violence, 2,888 show there is a direct correlation between watching violence on the screen and violence in real life.

In 2008, the Pew Research Center reported that 97 percent of children ages 12 to 17 play some type of video game and that two-thirds of those games are action and adventure games with violent content.[6] "Blood and gore. Intense violence. Strong sexual content. Use of drugs." These are just a few of the phrases that the Entertainment Software Rating Board (ESRB) uses to describe the content of these "games."

The vast majority of psychological studies on gaming show that video games increase aggressive behavior and increase negative thoughts and emotions in children, potentially leading to mental illness.[7] They also create a sense of distance from real life and an increasing numbness and lessened concern for others.

Considering the relentless focus on killing and violence, is it any wonder we neither remember nor act like Who We Really Are?

Create gladiators

There isn't much difference in training attack dogs and training soldiers by brutalizing them in basic training—dehumanizing and pitting them against one another, rewarding for aggression.

Ridley Scott's iconic film *Gladiator*, filmed in 2000, shows how easy it is to wrest a man from ethical rationality, hurling him into savagery. Slaughter his wife and child and sell him into slavery. Then put a sword in his hands and reward his pain-driven rage.

Tell a man his God is threatened. His home. His family. His people. His way of life. His most precious ideals. Teach him violence is not only acceptable but praiseworthy. Give him a gun and point him towards the "enemy"—the other guy who's been told his God, home, family, people, way of life, and most precious ideals are threatened—and watch what happens.

Turn men into unfeeling robots

Obviously, emotional and empathic castration are a vital part of creating effective warriors. At all cost, men's emotions must be switched off by equating emotions and any sense of compassion with weakness (IE. women). The more men are forced into battle and bloodshed, the more traumatized they become, the easier this process of emotional cauterization will be.

Implant a lust for rulership

The creation of an elite class is another dehumanizing tactic. Just as soldiers are taught contempt for the lives of others, so are most rulers. Whether the elevation occurs through bloodlines, (the Divine Right of Kings, God's Chosen Ones), birth as a man, priestly rank, or the acquisition of great material wealth, the end goal is the creation of rulership based in "power over others"— entitlement based in hierarchy and the belief that one human being is better than another.

Both rulers and the ruled are less than human in this creation.

Equality does not exist. Love is not only unnecessary, it impedes effective rulership. Ruthless cunning, aggression, competition, indifference to the wellbeing of others and the planet itself are key dynamics of this model.

Sound familiar?

Turn men into drones

If not a ruler or a warrior, a man is only useful as a means to an end. He is a tool. A drone. A worker in the mines and fields, offices and factories. A mindless cog in the consumer wheel. Cannon fodder. A number in a computer. A candidate for AI augmentation and ultimate control.

Modern educational and military models are perfectly designed to facilitate this social molding.

Turn men into caricatures of women

There is an obvious agenda afoot to confuse the modern male who, over countless generations, has been deliberately diminished and unbalanced via all the above methods. In his current off-kilter, numbed state, it's not hard to confuse and manipulate him.

And yet, men are spirits of pure love. Like women, they instinctively know something is horribly wrong. They know, deep down, that patriarchy is unbalanced and out of control. They know that THEY are unbalanced and out of control. As a result of this mostly unconscious knowing, it is only natural that men start to gravitate towards a more feminine-balanced expression, adopting more nurturing roles.

Which is an extremely healthy evolution for men.

Add to that natural evolution the fact that for the last 100 years women have also been shifting out of their own radically unbalanced state by adopting masculine characteristics and roles. This movement also presses more and more men to lean towards more yin expression.

Great! The beginnings of inner balance in everyone! Yay!

Unfortunately, women have been programmed to adopt and embody patriarchal values and qualities—twisted versions of the yang expression. Instead of moving into greater dynamic action, structure, one-pointed focus and transparency, women have been driven to express power-over dynamics, competition, ruthlessness, exploitation, control and overwork.

And the men? What kind of "feminine" yin expression are they being influenced to adopt?

Anheuser-Busch's Bud Lite commercials featuring transgender promoter Dylan Mulvaney give us the answer, and it is not the powerful, life-honoring yin values of empathy, connection, nurturing, and compassion that are being presented. Instead, an overly made-up Mulvaney simpers and flirts in a bubble bath while wearing clothes, brainlessly pretending to know nothing about "manly" issues like sports, all the while swigging low-calorie beer to keep her girlish figure intact.

Instead of genuine yang and yin energies, both men and women are being ruthlessly driven to adopt age-old caricatures of the opposite gender expression—ludicrous gender roles designed by the controllers. And it's working because people have zero awareness of what masculine/yang and feminine/yin even are.

The last thing the global elites want is a population of balanced, sane men and women expressing their full-spectrum humanity, going harmoniously about their lives in peace, full knowledge, and satisfied fulfillment.

Turn men into women

Depleted by being forced to play out the roles of ruler, power broker, warrior, drone and pawn, limited and depressed, stressed and maxed out, it isn't surprising that men are desperately seeking other, more creative expressions. And aside from the stereotypical caricature of a woman, what else is on public offer? What else is being crammed down men's throats by the media, educators, and the medical establishment?

The trans agendas. Men becoming women by swapping out body parts and hormones. Cross- dressing. Men with penises and beards wearing dresses and high heels. Gay men taking estrogen pretending to nurse adopted infants, ensuring early childhood trauma in the little ones. Children believing men can give birth and all sorts of other bizarre and ludicrous fantasies playing out on the world stage.

Turn men into robots

The other alternative soon to be on offer is a more digital, robotized existence as an extension of AI with brain-implant augmentation. And then, of course, there is always AI-assisted Virtual Reality—another level of distortion offering all sorts of unimaginably violent, cruel, and horrific scenarios to experience. A compressed 2D programming tool that eliminates the inconvenience of the human body and life altogether.

The alternative

There is an alternative to all of this. Thank God! There is a more-than-bright future waiting for humanity to create. But it takes knowledge—and then it takes the guts to act on the knowledge and walk a different path than the limited roles on offer being pushed by manipulated social media platforms, educators, politicians and global elites.

Best suggestion? Ditch the stupid roles.

To be a man and to be a woman is to live a balanced, rich, unlimited, full-spectrum life in all its flavors and nuances—including any and all gender/sexual expressions. This is the default setting of every individual on this planet.

War, confusion, despair, distortion, and pathology flow from agendas of control and manipulation. Once out of the programming box, the flowering of creativity born of freedom arises. Community, connection, cooperation, peace, healthy expansion spontaneously take root, crowding out dark influences and corrupt agendas until they are no more than vague memories of a bad dream in the night.

EXPLORATION

Poor men! What a terrible campaign has been waged to separate them from their humanity! And talk about sexual exploitation! We've been focused on women's exploitation for so long we've been blinded to what the guys have been going through.

They've had their yang energies—linear focus, strength, action, intellect, structure—grossly amplified, distorted, harnessed and fed upon by the Powers That Be ... yang energies that have been used to fuel the rise and fall of civilizations for thousands of years.

If women have been reduced to sex toys, men have been reduced to roboticized weapons of war and drones used for every type labor imaginable.

But, if this is true, why are men apparently being "softened up" lately?

Is it, perhaps, because of the rise of AI and the coming availability of robot armies and laser-based weaponry? Do the Powers That Be now need a more placid, pliable, controllable army of pseudo men? What other possibility is there?

Chapter 9

The Myth of Patriarchy

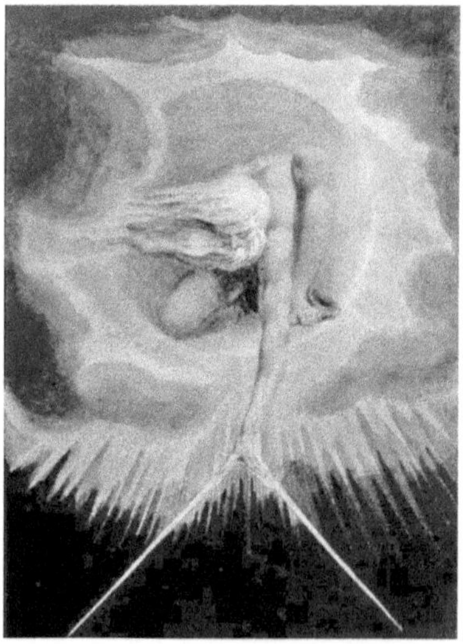

Few images are more esoterically revealing than 18th century British poet and artist William Blake's painting "Urizen," aka The Great Architect. I always thought the centuries-old work of art cleverly showed God creating the world by creating duality via electromagnetic polarity—the negative yin force and the positive yang force, so labeled by Eastern science. But then back in the 1700s, nobody knew that negative and positive electromagnetic charges existed, let alone that they were the foundation upon which physical worlds and human bodies are built. Or that these "first creations" came into being less a second after the Big Bang occurred.

As it turns out, however, even though it's not about God, the image is indeed telling a creation story. Just not the creation I originally thought.

Blake, a member of the Masonic Swedenborgian Theosophical Society, which he joined in the 1780s, used this image to illustrate his mythic tale, "Urizen," describing the fall of mankind into the clutches of satanic forces and how people subsequently created a limited world of "divided light" based in rationality, rule, and science, in which everyone—man and woman alike— became helplessly trapped and depleted.

Sound familiar?

The image itself depicts man's creation of the draftsman's compass—a Masonic symbol for rationalism and rule over the emotional/physical world through logic and science. An image that couldn't be more perfect to go with a commentary on patriarchy.

What is patriarchy?

According to *The American Heritage Dictionary*, 5th edition, patriarchy is: "A social system in which the father is the head of the family. A family, community, or society based on this system or governed by men. Dominance of a society by men, or the values that uphold such dominance."

Up until a couple years ago, I thought men were responsible for patriarchal dominance on this planet. I mean, it's obvious. Sure, we women let it all happen. But we were overpowered by the greedy, violent, controlling dudes. Right?

But then COVID came along in 2020 and I had to rethink global reality. Researching and writing the book *Cracking the Matrix*, I discovered that the world's current condition isn't the men's fault. Or the women's fault either. Blake's story told the truth. Humanity, as a whole, has been incessantly beleaguered and driven towards destruction by what has been labeled "satanic" intelligences and their possessed human puppets for thousands of years.

Which is not to say we haven't all been complicit. For thousands of years humanity, as a collective, has been greedy and thoughtless, blind, stupid, cruel, self-serving and short-sighted, naive, gullible and easily manipulated. We have been all of that and more. But we are NOT to blame for everything that's gone down— including the creation of patriarchy.

The "Dominance of a society by men, or the values that uphold such dominance" is a construct flowing from the minds of those who, as Blake illustrated, have fallen into the clutches of a negative interdimensional consciousness, hallmarked by arrogance, pride, contempt, divisiveness, cruelty and debauchery. A consciousness which has insinuated itself into the minds and bodies of the weak and the avaricious for a very long time. And through these human marionettes has managed to degrade our reality, steadily diminishing and crushing us into a matrix of mindless materiality. Bottomline:

Patriarchy is the deliberate exaggeration and defilement of the masculine/yang principle by design of elitist factions as a method of division, conflict and control.

If we take the energetic qualities of the positive electromagnetic charge and completely divorce them from the qualities and influence of the negative electromagnetic charge, it's easy to see how the qualities of hardness, pointedness, externality, linearity, action, guardedness, structure, fixedness, singularity, isolation, and light can become exaggerated and ultimately destructive.

Once successfully isolated and unbalanced, the quality of hardness that permits rocks and mountains to exist can become impenetrable, unyielding inflexibility. Linearity, fixedness, and action can create a tidal wave of unstoppable destruction that takes out everything in its path. Structure, deliberately pushed to extremes and elevated above organic fluidity and intuition, builds a prison. Logic without love chains us to the prison walls. The social construct we experience today called patriarchy has resulted from the deliberate over exaggeration and elevation of the qualities defining the masculine/yang principle with the intended purpose of creating exactly what we have today: an unbalanced, materialistic, driven, self-destructive, highly-sexed society that has no soul, no joy, no love, no compassion, no respect for life, and no "OFF" switch.

Back to patriarchy

I've been aware of much of this programming since the mid 1980s. But it had zero chance of actually affecting my day-to-day existence because my day-to-day existence occluded its importance. I was too busy getting ahead in my media career. Too busy meditating. Too busy trying to pay the bills. Too busy with my relationships.

I was too busy drinking booze—trying to find relief from all the pressure and anxiety my life contained as I perpetuated the dream spun by the global elites—to actually believe any "conspiracy crap," let alone do something about it.

Now, all these years later, I'm finally out of the matrix. I'm not interested in pursuing the life I was programmed to pursue anymore. My time is no longer absorbed by the lies and distractions, mindless entertainment and propaganda sending me down the cattle chute chasing "success" and non-existent "security" and all that implies.

Instead of desperately trying to secure my place in a deadly paradigm designed to hypnotize and suck me dry, I spend my time examining the matrix, disentangling myself while trying to find ways to describe it so other people can see it and escape its clutches as well.

But once we are out, what then?

Perspective

I'm not saying personal gender issues don't exist. I'm saying they are deliberately blown out of proportion and weaponized. I'm not saying people don't suffer over their identity. Almost everybody suffers over their identity on this planet because our true identity has been deliberately obscured and our focus aimed towards obsessive identification with the body and material wealth—IE. "things" that can be used and messed with.

Lost in the matrix, confused about Who We Really Are, eager to jump on the next bandwagon hoping it will give us a purpose and a sense of "self," we're sitting ducks for mental and emotional manipulation.

People are in pain—massive pain—desperate for meaning and direction. And then psyops organizations manipulate that pain via social media algorithms and commercial media. Which is why social issues—pro-gay, bi, trans, BLM, feminist, Hamas, Israel, Ukraine, whatever—are now appearing on the world stage as full-blown social movements, seemingly overnight.

Our pain is being fed upon and directed in ways designed to amplify that pain and create even more.

Is it easy seeing this? Am I saying "Hey, just wake up and get over yourselves?" God, no. Waking up means more pain on top of pain—at least temporarily. But then, once you start to grasp what's really going on, the deepest wounds start to heal. The massive internal agony of not knowing self and not trusting self, begins to subside.

Confusion evaporates as the light of truth warms your heart. "It's not my fault! I've been tricked!" Flickers of inner direction grow, until light dawns and it's a new day and a new reality and a new world.

Does everybody get a hall pass for all the crap we've helped create over the millennia by supporting the matrix programs we've bought into and been trapped in? Programs like patriarchy? Yes, we do. You can't blame ignorant people for what they do out of ignorance.

However, once the light begins to dawn, STOP.

Step back from being so caught up and identified with divisive issues deliberately created to do us all harm. Stop participating. Get out from underneath the vampiric agenda of the interdimensional and human controllers.

Take responsibility and take back your power.

Game over

Once we see the Great Lie that's being perpetrated upon us—that we are the ones who are weak, that we are the ones who are so foul and so confused that we need strict governing and control to ensure our very species' survival—once we see this is all a terrible nightmare we've bought into and supported ... we are free.

Free to have the time and opportunity to pick up the pieces

and start reassessing Who We Really Are. Free to be loving and kind. Free to be compassionate. Free to respect all of life. Free to spread our wings to create and then implement the awesome inventions and systems that can clean up our planet, that can healthily feed everyone, that can restore health and wellbeing to all. Free to pursue individual happiness—not at the expense of others—but alongside others.

The future is awesome and bright. We are coming out of the Valley of the Shadow of Death and we need have no fear of evil. For we are beings of pure love who shine far too brightly for the shadows to gather around us anymore.

EXPLORATION

It is shocking how many things, once tarred with the "conspiracy" brush, have now been proven true. For example, the Manhattan Project was called a conspiracy theory before the truth came out with the US bombing of Hiroshima in Japan at the end of World War II.

The US government running massive mind control experiments on US and Canadian citizens was considered a conspiracy theory until the US government's program MK-Ultra was exposed via the Freedom of Information Act in 1977 and subsequently investigated in formal Senate hearings. For decades the CIA conducted mind control experiments through American universities and hospitals. The CIA also kidnapped men—American citizens—out of brothels and flophouses, dosed them with LSD and tortured them to see how far they could be pushed past their mental and moral limits. Additional documentation on the program was released in 2001. As well, the CIA's covert operation to control the media by planting stories and manipulating the news was exposed in the 1970s.

The derogatory "conspiracy" label employed by the mainstream media is wearing thin as more and more info is exposed by people like Julian Assange, Robert F. Kennedy, Jr., David Icke and Tucker Carlson.

So, if you're interested in diving deeper down various rabbit holes, the following is a brief listing of books to give you a start. It is astounding how well researched and footnoted these sources are and how much cold, hard proof there is available to us, if we only bother to look

- *State of War: The Secret History of the CIA and the Bush Administration,* James Risen, Free Press, (2006)
- *The Art of War*, by Sun Tzu, Fingerprint! Publishing (December, 2018)
- *The Biggest Secret: The Book That Will Change the World,* David Icke, David Icke Books; 2nd Updated ed. edition (January, 1999)
- *The Creature from Jekyll Island* by G. Edward Griffin, American Media; 5th edition (January, 2010)
- *The Great Reset: Joe Biden and the Rise of Twenty-First-Century Fascism,* Glenn Beck, Forefront Books (January, 2022)
- *The Real Anthony Fauci: Bill Gates, Big Pharma, and the Global War on Democracy and Public Health,* Robert F. Kennedy Jr., Simon & Schuster (2021
- *The Trap: What It Is, How It Works, and How We Escape Its Illusions,* David Icke Books, (September, 2022)
- *The Unseen Hand: An Introduction to the Conspiratorial View of History* by Ralph Epperson, Publius Press (1985)

Chapter 10

Weaponing Gender

At age ten, I asked my mother how babies are made. Being rather puritanical and easily embarrassed, the only thing she said was, "Oh, for heaven's sake, Cate! Just go out and watch the cows."

I was raised on a big farm in Virginia, so following her advice was easy. And what I observed was: 1) the neutered steers (males) humped the other steers. 2) The steers humped the heifers (the young females). 3) The heifers humped the steers and other heifers. 4) The bull humped and impregnated the mature cows. 5) Everybody did it dog-style.

To say my sexual orientation was fluid and liberal growing up because of this education is an understatement. As a result, I have no issues with gays, bi-sexuals, trans-sexuals or any other kind of sexual. How somebody expresses their personal nature and uses their body (as long as it's consensual)—however they feel, however they identify, and however they are attracted and act on those feelings and identifications—is their business. Not mine.

Until, that is, various factions make their business my business by distorting sex, sexuality, and gender, politicizing and manipulating people and issues, creating global problems and divisiveness to suit a demonic globalist agenda.

Then I get involved. And pick up my (virtual) pen.

An artificial issue

Cows, giraffes, gorillas, lions, manatees, humans—in the last three million years there's probably not a species on Earth that hasn't mixed it up plenty, sexually speaking. As mental, emotional, spiritual, and physical beings, humans are multidimensional in nature, and it is possible to be attracted to and procreate with the opposite sex, to align with no gender at all, or both genders, or even identify as the other gender. In Native American tradition "two-spirit" men and women who easily crossed sexual boundaries were considered advanced beings who had basically transcended their biology.

People have been loving the opposite sex, identifying as the opposite sex, loving the same sex, identifying as no sex, and God-knows-what sex for millions of years. It's no big deal.

Until it's deliberately made into a big deal.

Which is what happened when the followers of Abraham were coached into creating the third book of the Torah known as the Book of Leviticus—a book of rules written around 1400 BC that the ancient Jews believed they had to follow in order to please God—a book with a rule forbidding homosexuality as "against God's order of things."

Actually, all three world religions founded upon Abrahamic principles—Judaism, Islam and Christianity—judge and denounce homosexuality. (For that matter, all three religions make sex and pleasure questionable pursuits no matter who's doing what to whom—baby-making, of course, being the sole and whole-heartedly approved exception.)

Buddha said nothing on the topic of sexuality—no matter what brand—in any of his lengthy discourses. For him, it obviously wasn't an issue worth mentioning.

Just part of the agenda

I could go off on a huge riff here about ancient aliens and genetic experiments on early humans in the Middle East and African continent by a race of extraterrestrials known as the Anunnaki attempting to create a slave race ... which, if it's true, lends credibility to "god" exhorting Adam and Eve to go off and "be fruitful and multiply." (We want more slaves available to do our bidding!)

Surely the rules in Leviticus and the Quran forbidding homosexuality would make total sense given such a context.

But instead, I'll simply remind the reader that there is a long-term agenda inimical to the wellbeing of humanity being pushed by forces whose job it is to incite conflict between human beings, wherever and however possible on this planet. Turning pleasure (who doesn't want that?) and sex—the major, unstoppable biological driving force for humanity—into a socio-religious battleground is like shooting fish in a barrel.

If somebody wanted to guarantee shame, guilt and angst on a grand scale amongst humans on this planet (after already creating an appalling conflict between man and woman), "dirtifying" sex and outlawing homosexuality and other forms of non-binary expression would most decidedly accomplish the task.

Trans: The latest gender attack

Fostering religious shame around sex has created endless pathological issues and trauma in most of humanity. Vilifying homosexuality, bi-sexuality, pan-sexuality etc. has caused horrific suffering, conflict, and outright murder.

The latest media-hyped gender attack by the Controllers manages to deliver us conflict, PLUS the twin specters of sexual mutilation/neutering and depopulation, all at the expense of individuals identifying as trans.

According to the 2013 Diagnostic and Statistical Manual of Mental Disorders, Fifth Edition, the prevalence of gender dysphoria averages around 0.005–0.014 percent of the population. Prior to 1980, the DSM made no reference to gender identity at all.[8] It just wasn't on anybody's radar, and dysphoric "onsets" that were recorded usually occurred at or before age seven and involved mostly males.

Fast forward *eight years* and in 2021 alone, in the US about 42,000 children ages six to 17 received a diagnosis of gender dysphoria, nearly triple the number in 2017.[9] Teen girls with no history of gender dysphoria started identifying as boys in about 60 percent of these cases.[10] (Of course, this trending preference for being a guy couldn't possibly have anything to do with sexual discrimination against women for the last 5,000 years?)

Coincidentally, the trans movement is a veritable gold mine as far as economics is concerned, because transgender people require drugs and medical treatments for the rest of their lives.

In the mid-1990s there were two "gender clinics" in North America. Today, there are over four hundred. The sex reassignment market in the United States, practically non-existent ten years ago, was worth $1.9 billion in 2021, and is expected to grow by as much as 11 percent annually.[11] The medical establishment is estimated to make $1.4 million over the course of the life of every child who medically transitions. Lupron, a drug now being prescribed as a puberty blocker, earned the pharmaceutical manufacturer AbbVie $726 million in 2018 alone. Side effects include allergic reactions, chest pain, breathing problems, depression, memory loss, severe headache, visual problems and vomiting.

Dr. Miriam Grossman, a child and adolescent psychiatrist and board-certified medical doctor, says she suspects that most college, high school and elementary school students now believe that sex and gender are two separate things, and that you can choose your gender at will.

They believe it because the propaganda is everywhere. Even English language dictionaries are being changed to suit the "fluid gender agenda." Twenty years ago. *The Cambridge English Dictionary* defined gender as being "the condition of being physically male or female." Today the primary definition of gender is: "A group of people in a society who share particular qualities or ways of behaving which that society associates with being male, female, or another identity."

Gender is now a "group of people" that "share qualities" that society "associates" with male and female or some "other identity." (Arcturian? Atlantean? Pleiadian? What?) And the belief that you can choose your gender depending on your emotional issues (welcome to puberty) and the social influences of the moment is being presented over and over in a million different ways as "fact."

The ability and the right to choose your gender identity is presented in such a way that if you question the validity of this "fact," then you're obviously transphobic and a bad person and someone no one should listen to.

Today, we have young people marching, demanding trans rights, and legislators making hay on trans issues. Female Olympic athletes who have dedicated their lives to their sport are brutalized and beaten by trans competitors in every area in which they compete.

Women's safety zones are rapidly being threatened as bus

stations, airports and restaurants race to relabel bathroom doors before they get sued. Transvestites in full drag are reading children's books to little ones in kindergartens and daycare centers. We have laws being passed that keep parents from interfering with their underage children choosing puberty blockers and sex-reassignment surgeries that could mutilate and castrate them for life.

It's a world gone gender mad.

Are there little boys and little girls sometimes born who truly know they're in the wrong sex body like my client Carl? Absolutely. Does it help some to transition physically? Absolutely. Should they be supported and respected for their choices? Absolutely. Is the epidemic of gender dysphoria sweeping youth—especially youth in America—a true biological evolution? No.

The fact that the rates of gender dysphoria are directly proportional to the popularity and availability of media and social media programming makes this highly suspect. But at this point, the issue is so fraught, so contentious, the smoke and mirrors tap dance by educators, psychologists, doctors, and the media so overwhelming, the voices shouting from so many disparate directions, it's hard to tell what is truly going on.

But life's mandate is supporting and encouraging more life. Global gender confusion and mass neutering is hardly in alignment with that.

But if not, then why—aside from young people's wise desire to not be stuck in an utterly false, binary reality—is this movement occurring? To what end?

The weaponization of sex

The game of divide and conquer is a no-holds-barred event. You attack where your opponent is weakest. You hit below the belt. You grab 'em by the crown jewels and squeeze.

Weaponizing sex started out as a game of simple gender division—a relatively straightforward matter of devising various means of keeping men and women at each other's throats. But men and women aren't just men and women. We are multidimensional beings. We are spiritual, mental, emotional and biological beings who are naturally social beings. We're wired all sorts of different ways. Which means there are many different avenues and levels of expression, and therefore many different avenues and levels of attack—many different ways to create judgment, discrimination, and division.

It also means there are just as many different ways we can all eventually come to understanding and healing. But to come to healing we have to be willing to tackle and talk about difficult subjects. And gender is so fraught! How many different ways will I offend how many different people in these pages?

But if we don't bring everything out in the open—if we refuse to take a Big Picture, multidimensional approach to sensitive subjects and see what's really going on—well, then, the results don't bear thinking about.

And if there's anybody reading this who still feels a little tender around the subject of sex, gender, homosexuality, lesbianism, trans identity, bi-sexuality or anything else in the sex arena, try not to get too uptight. Left unmolested and unagendized, sexuality in all its healthy, playful forms is natural.

And if you need a reminder, just go out and watch the cows.

EXPLORATION

This is an emotionally charged, politically incorrect chapter. And I didn't mean to seem cavalier when I ended it with a prompting to go out and watch the cows. But it actually is my best advice to go outside and seriously contemplate nature for awhile.

Observe how everything in nature is in order. Observe how everything works seamlessly. Harmoniously. Observe how reliable and steadfast nature is in being itself.

There is an intelligence in nature—an intelligence we are part of—that supersedes intellect and logic. Nature is so much smarter than us! But we're lost in the delusion and arrogance of the mind and mental processes. We're programmed to see ourselves as separate. Better. Superior. To see nature as a primitive, violent, untrustworthy, dog-eat-dog environment.

And yet what can you trust more? Governments and corporations and armies? Or nature?

Nature has so much to teach us about Who We Really Are. And it's a beautiful message. A message that takes us out of the battlefield of the mind driving vacillating public opinions, memes, marches, flag waving, protests and name calling, bringing us back to ourselves.

My point is this: The only disturbing element on this planet is human beings. Not nature. And if your next thought is that humans, *by nature,* are screwed up. Think again. That's the program we've been sold.

Our nature is pure love. Nature's nature is pure love/life force intelligence. What's screwed up is the propaganda being shoved down our throats 24/7 and all the agendas that keep us divided, confused and miserable.

A nature story

Most of my friends have heard me marvel at the resilience and tenacity of life. I've watched little flowers push up towards the light between cracks in cement. Seen human bodies keep going long after I thought it was possible for them to sustain another breath.

Frankly, given the horrific levels of chemical and biological pollutants in the air, water, and food supply—the poisonous pharmaceutical load, the destructive electromagnetic fields, the vicious psychological programming—it stuns me that a human being can stay alive let alone healthy past age 20.

Seriously! The fact that we do goes to prove my point that life is obviously vastly more intelligent, complex, and resilient than humans tend to realize or even want to admit.

The truth of the matter is: Life is infinite and eternal.

To this incomprehensible infinitude we bring our grasshopper-like perspective. We dissect things under microscopes and peer through telescopes, do dangerous gain-of-function experiments on bat corona viruses in leaky laboratories, and make up wonderful theories to explain different aspects of life. But we're still very much the proverbial blind men, feeling up an elephant.

An elephant the size of the multiverse.

Unfortunately, instead of wisely expending our energies expanding our consciousness in an effort to be equal to the gobsmacking magnificence we're part of, in our pride, humanity has taken the exact opposite tack. We've reduced the magnitude and magnificence of the beast that confronts us. Made life small and predictable. Manageable. Controlled by Darwinian Theory and hydroelectric dams, Newtonian physics and pharmaceuticals.

Lost in a delusional bubble of intellectualism and reductionist thinking, we believe we've got a handle on the nature of the elephant. And yet, truth be told, we haven't got a clue what we're dealing with. We have almost zero understanding about how—or why—life works.

Let me give a couple examples that show what I mean.

The boy, the fish, and the eagle

Viktor Schauberger was a naturalist and forester's son who lived in early 20th century Austria. A profound observer of nature, he was a genius at hydroengineering and the multifaceted nature of water. While still a very young man, he was sitting by a lake one day, watching an eagle circle over the water in an ever-tighter spiral.

As he tracked the bird's shadow on the water, he realized there was a huge fish following the eagle's shadow, spiraling towards the surface of the lake as the eagle circled ever lower. It was, he observed, as if the fish were hypnotized by the bird's flight, tracking it exactly until the final moment when the fish swam right up to the surface and the eagle grabbed it in its talons.

Marveling at what he'd just witnessed, the young Schauberger watched in admiration as the eagle flew off with its tasty prize,

But that's not the end of the story. Years later, Schauberger found himself sitting by yet another pristine alpine lake watching yet another large fish swim in an ever-tightening circle. Looking up, he expected to see an eagle doing its hypnotist thing in the air above the lake. But there wasn't a bird in sight.

Puzzled, he continued to watch the fish circle. Eventually ... an eagle appeared on the horizon.

The dance repeated itself. Except this time, Schauberger

realized the roles were reversed from his original assumption. The fish had obviously called the eagle to it. Moving closer to the water, he watched the dance's denouement closely. At the last moment *the fish launched itself out of the water up into the extended talons of the eagle.*

Keystone species

After long contemplation, the best explanation Schauberger could come up with regarding the fish's astonishing display was: The fish was ready to evolve. The fish was ready to take on a new life expression. And the eagle was its key to that next higher experience.

Which completely rearranges our human perception of nature as this scary predatory environment, "red in tooth and claw," solely based on survival of the fittest. In this new view of species relationship, all predators aren't out randomly savaging and killing other animals. Some—known as keystone species—are consuming out of hunger while simultaneously ascending their prey into a higher order of life.

Keystone species open the door to higher-level expressions in more ways than one. By their very nature, the world around a keystone species improves with its presence. For example, wolves are a keystone species. Their reintroduction into an ecosystem results in an almost shockingly swift improvement in local species' health and variation—animals, plants, trees—right down to microorganism levels improving soil fertility and water quality.

Apparently, wolves offer their prey the same "upwardly mobile" services as eagles.

Our lost role

Once upon a time, when humans served as stewards of the Earth rather than rapacious land barons and abusers, we were a keystone species as well. Today, that ancient role is hardly known about, let alone enacted. But there are exceptions and some tribal communities still consciously maintain the role. I have been blessed to directly know about one.

Back in 1999 I worked as the NW editor and bureau chief for the national Native American newspaper *Indian Country Today*. During my time at the paper, the Makah Indian tribe of NW Washington State attempted to reintroduce its ancient whale hunting tradition after a 70-year ban—where one canoe with ten young male tribal members would set out into the rough seas of winter to take the life of one migrating grey whale, bringing back food and whale bone and oil to the tribe.

The world was outraged by the Makah tribe's decision and obvious lack of environmental ethics.

Never mind Japan commercially slaughters hundreds of whales each year—environmental protestors attacked the tribe. Greenpeace boats patrolled Pacific waters off the Washington coast, determined to ward off or even ram the canoe if it came anywhere near a whale. Hundreds of people gathered outside the reservation borders, waving signs. Death threats were made on the young hunters and their family members.

It was a zoo, and no news crews or reporters were allowed onto the res ... no one except me. Working for a Native paper, I was granted an exclusive interview with KeithJohnson, head of the Makah Whaling Commission. And instead of bothering him with newsy questions about the death threats and legal rights to hunt, I asked him about the tribe's whaling tradition.

Turns out Keith's son was the captain of the whaling canoe that, despite the furor, was daily plying the terrifying winter seas in search of a whale. Keith himself had been trained to perform this task ... as had his father before him in a long line of ancestors.

As Keith talked it became clear that the hunt was not just a "hunt." It was a sacred ritual and the enactment of an ages-old pact between the tribe and the grey whales.

He explained that the captain of the canoe was trained to *hear the call and connect with the spirit of a grey whale willing and ready to give its body for the tribe's sustenance.* In return for its body, the spirit of the whale would be escorted by the captain of the canoe to a "new shore" where it would be welcomed and born into the tribe in a human body.

Hello?

It was a deliberate act by a keystone species (humans of the Makah nation) enabling a member of another species to elevate itself into a new life—nothing less than the transmutation of a whale's spirit that was ready to become human—just like the fish was ready to become an eagle and fly.

Endless magic, endless life

We think we know everything there is to know about life. We think "God" put us here to do with the Earth what we will. We think we can manage and control nature. We think we have the power to destroy it. We think the environment is on the verge of collapse and that we have the power to save it.

I used to think that.

But stories like those above have jolted me out of the illusion that humanity knows what's going on into the realization that we know squat about nature and "the environment" and our place within it. Even if planet Earth were vaporized tomorrow, life/nature would go on and on and on ... just elsewhere and without you and me.

I tell these two tales to give some perspective on the topic of human nature and where and how we fit into the scheme of things. Nature has more going for it than we know and so do we.

As I said earlier in this chapter, there's probably not a species on Earth that hasn't mixed it up plenty, sexually speaking. People have been loving the opposite sex, identifying as the opposite sex, loving the same sex, identifying as no sex, and God-knows-what sex for millions of years. It's totally natural. It's no big deal.

Until it's deliberately made into a big deal.

The sooner all of humanity wakes up to the lies, twists and manipulations that have turned everything—including sexuality—into a gladiator event where people are driven to fight to the death over made-up issues, the better.

Chapter 11

Biology, Identity & Human Rights

When the 3.2-million-year-old fossilized bones of "Lucy," a female member of the hominin species Australopithecus afarensis were unearthed in Ethiopia in 1974, anthropologists knew the bones either belonged to a female or a hominin male. No other options were on the table.

When Noah was instructed to load up the ark, heaven help him if he'd gotten it wrong and picked giraffes, lions and gorillas that only identified as male and female, dressing and expressing the part.

Through a mirror darkly

Identity, by its very nature, is conceptual, subjective, and often highly influenced by external circumstances as well as internal sensibilities. In the 70s, 80s and 90s, I identified as a highly liberated woman. Yet, the truth of the matter is I was grotesquely influenced by my social environment to think of myself in those terms. In reality, I had never been more profoundly shackled and controlled.

Identity and a sense of self are two different things. The former is, again, rooted in the mind (which is easily subject to programming). The other is a matter of energetic awareness. Which makes total sense since, in reality, we are energy beings and not really physical at all.

If you close your eyes and simply tune into an awareness of your pure being outside of mind chatter, unless you're in pain, there is really no "thing" there except a sense of spaciousness and an awareness of being aware.

This is the real "you."

Which is why people at age seventy look in the mirror and can't believe their eyes. Where did the time go? And who is that wrinkled old person staring back at them from the mirror? Their inner sense of "self"—that inner spaciousness—is the same at 70 as it was at 40, at 20, and at age five.

But the mirror!

Ah ... the mirror is one of the reasons why we wrestle so fiercely with the idea of death and fear it so much. We identify with the image we see in the glass. We identify with bodies that aren't really physical but seem so because of sensory input from the body itself. But we also identify with being limited and mortal because exterior input tells us who we are.

Genuine trans individuals like my client Carl clearly sense a distinct energetic mismatch between their spirit's essence and the energetic garment they wear long before physical sensory data—both from the body and external sources—finishes informing them of the situation.

Self is spirit.
Identity is an idea about the "physical" self.

Identity versus reality

When transgender issues first started being seriously talked about ten or so years ago, I had a couple trans friends who did hormone therapy but who never physically transitioned via surgery. They eventually dumped the hormone therapy because it wrecked havoc on their bodies and emotional wellbeing.

They were both born male but identified as female and lesbian. There didn't seem to be a whole lot of issues around sexual identity for them. (At least we didn't talk about it.) And I simply accepted them as they are—two intelligent, kind, human beings I enjoyed hanging out with who wore male bodies that they were doing their best to remold into a more feminine model that suited them better as they went about living a lesbian lifestyle that matched their individual, personal identities.

Myself, I was delighted by the concept of "gender fluidity" when it came along, because it substantiated my long-held spiritual understanding that we humans are far more than just our physical bodies. I thought that identifying with a state other than the body's actual sex was indicating a growing awareness of humanity's overarching spiritual nature. An evolutionary awareness that would help get humanity out of its obsessive fixation on the body, consumeristic materialism, and an overall limited expression in life.

Not so. As the whole trans issue became ever-more notorious, it became obvious that young people were becoming even more obsessed and more narrowly identified with their bodies and sexual expression than ever.

"Biological identity" is the foundation for the whole trans movement. Okay. Identify away. But then I started hearing that young people were starting to believe that having a certain gender identity meant that they were actually now the sex they identified with. That their belief made it so and that they should now be accorded automatic rights and legal status that aligned with their *belief*. I was even hearing that many young people actually believed (and were being taught) that men who identified as women could become pregnant and have babies.

Which is obviously delusional.

Why, in the name of political correctness, are educational and medical experts and establishments now supporting and even encouraging delusional behavior?

An offensive meme

Some time ago, somebody sent me a trans-oriented meme. After considerable internal debate, I posted it on Facebook—not because I thought it was funny (I didn't), and certainly not because I wanted to hurt some people's feelings. I posted it because my desire to stimulate a lucid conversation around the gender insanity being perpetrated outweighed my sense of political correctness.

The same is still true. So here I go, talking about it again.

Outrage

The meme showed trans swimmer Lia Thomas next to a dolled-up Lynda Carter and said: "My generation had Wonder Woman. Your generation has 'Wonder if it's a woman?'"

Predictably, the post got major pushback. One reader wrote: "Bigotry isn't witty, cute or funny. You're a better person than to post something like this." Another commented: "I don't find this humorous. For those who are insisting that only those who are assigned female at birth truly have the right to identify as women, you are missing the mark. Using the word 'it'? WTF?"

In response, I said I believed anybody could identify any way they wanted. But that didn't change their biological reality. For heaven's sake, Carl, who most certainly identifies as masculine and who has completed transitioned by carving up his body surgically to attain physiological maleness, understands that he is "trans" and not a "man." He knows he will never be a real "man" except in his mind, with his body attaining the most genuine facsimile possible through medical intervention.

I also said I posted the meme because I thought it was a message worth talking about. That the sentiments it expresses directly speak to millions of people's perceptions around the enormous gender issues being thrown at us.

I asked: "Are the very real, lived perceptions and thoughts of masses of people not supposed to be expressed because some people might find them offensive?"

To the "woke" crowd, of course, the answer was and is a vociferous and violent "YES!" A sentiment opined by every radically self-centered religious and political cult that has ever wrecked havoc across the annals of human history.

Biology vs identification

But let's put aside the issue of freedom of thought and speech for a moment.

Just because I identify as a sexy 29-year-old doesn't take me back four decades in time and make me 29 again. (Dammit!) I can do hormone replacement therapy and erase my wrinkles with Botox, dye my hair and shop at Forever 21 and hang out at the mall ... but that doesn't make me 29.

Does this rude biological fact cause me pain and suffering? Actually, I confess that it does.

From a purely physical perspective, getting older sucks. Not only is the body subject to more aches and pains and stiffness, I live in a shallow society that values youth and physical beauty above all things except money. As an older woman I am not just marginalized—I am rendered invisible. I can hear the words now: "Oh God! I'm so sorry I ran over you with my ______ (fill in the blank: shopping cart/golf cart/automobile.) I just didn't see you standing there!"

I turned male heads for decades. Now? Nada. And yes, that hurts. But what's worse is I truly feel 29. (Well, maybe 35.) The real me is ageless. Perpetually young and vibrant and beautiful. Why can't people (men) see that anymore? Sigh.

Am I free to pretend I'm still biologically 29? Am I free to get plastic surgery and wear miniskirts? Absolutely. Are people going to judge me for my Botox-stretched face, dress-style, and actions? Most likely. Will some people say mean things? Most likely. Although probably behind my back.

Is it going to be fun knowing that some people will laugh at me? No. But that's just life. Sometimes it's hard. Sometimes our choices reap unpleasant consequences—especially when they take us up against mainstream consensus reality.

Does my being hurt by others' opinions give me the right to shut them down, make them wrong and require them to shut up? Attack people who post memes about mutton being dressed up as lamb?

I might wish it were so. But the answer is plainly "No."

Human rights

In the Facebook conversation, I received posts saying things like: "People that are in their 60s and act 20 do not suffer the same persecution and misunderstanding as trans people. Your human rights are not threatened. It is not the same argument."

Well, let's look at this.

Some of the synonyms for "persecution" include the words "ill-treatment, oppression, exile, and murder." Would you consider being treated as a non-entity, being automatically dismissed as irrelevant and senile because you have wrinkles and grey hair, basically being viewed as if you have no physical or mental capacity "ill-treatment and oppression?"

How about "exile?"

Most certainly, in the West, elders are misunderstood and consigned to the hinterlands as far as relevance is concerned. Certainly the "woke" crowd doesn't consider older peoples' outdated, old-fashioned opinions and sentiments as valid.

What about murder? Well, all I can say is, it's pretty damn soul-killing being viewed and treated as an invisible, irrelevant fossil just because of your age. But let's move on and ask ourselves: What are the most important basic human rights?

In the US we're used to hearing the answer "life, liberty and the pursuit of happiness." Personally, I believe we are ALL in terrible danger of losing all three of these inalienable human rights. But I'll pass on that political hot potato for the moment and point a few other things out instead.

Humanity still hasn't advanced in consciousness to the point where food and shelter and safety are considered basic human rights—which IMO is unconscionable. I would also say that basic human rights to clean water, clean food, clean air and health care are inarguable—although many argue.

In the realm of socio-political rights, the Equal Rights Amendment, first introduced to Congress in 1923 to give equal rights to women, STILL has not been ratified in 100 years. Why? The excuse is it is now presumed that all people are considered equal. That sufficient safeguards are in place guaranteeing women's rights and that it's not an issue anymore.

Which is patently not true.

Women still don't get paid the same amount of money for the same job as men after 100 years of trying! And now we're at the point of not being able to gather safely as women. I used to belong to a Korean Woman's health spa. It was lovely being able to soak naked, get a massages and a facial, just relaxing around other women. But they recently had to close the spa down because the owners refused to allow men identifying as women to join.

Soon, women won't be able to take their pants down and pee in a public restroom anymore without biological males (supposedly) identifying as female around.

Talk about violating basic human rights ... and dignity!

A little common sense, please

Black people, White people, Red, Yellow and Brown people, gay people, trans people, people with special needs—ALL have the same basic HUMAN rights, (or they damn well should) which are what I stated before: Life, liberty and the pursuit of happiness. Access to food, shelter, safety, clean water, clean air, clean food and healthcare.

How about we take care of the most basic of rights that are pertinent to ALL humans and not get side-tracked by issues like public recognition of my personal identity as a woman or a man and having my personal pronouns agreed with and granted by all?

This is not to say that trans people aren't marginalized, demeaned and hurt in this world. They are. But they don't have the corner on the market. So are women. So are children with Downs Syndrome. So are Blacks and Native Americans and every other person of color. Even White males are now getting bashed. This doesn't make any of it right. Frankly, it's ironic to realize that about the only thing everyone seems to have a "right" to on this planet at the moment is the right to be hurt.

It's going to take some serious growing up on all our parts—some serious, edgy-yet-non- threatening conversations like this one that are open to exploring the human condition—so that we can unreservedly find our way forward to creating a world that is designed to work for the honor and benefit of all by all. In other words: How about a little common sense and concern for the welfare of humanity? And how about asking ourselves who benefits the most by keeping people focused on subjective individual issues—a guaranteed basis for chronic disagreement and division?

Who benefits by keeping us traumatized, thin-skinned, easily triggered and wounded? Who benefits most by keeping us all on edge and pissed at each other, preoccupied with pronouns and the labels of 80+ genders instead of tending to the Big Picture?

Hmmmm ... I wonder.

EXPLORATION

A lot of friends have told me they've been attacked for saying things like "All lives matter" in public and online. This statement is seen as a racist remark that is basically spitting in the face of Blacks and trans, bi and gay people, negating their marginalization, their pain and the prejudicial issues they're facing and trying to rectify.

The implied context to this is that women and men—in particular Caucasian women and men—have had it so good for so long and are so entitled that they deserve all the backlash they've got coming to them. They've been at the top of the heap, stomping everybody else flat for thousands of years, it's time they got put in their place and made room for others.

Now, I'm NOT saying people of color and non-binary people haven't been suppressed and oppressed and attacked and vilified by Whites. They have. But I would hope by this point you will have realized that all of this is part of The Program that's been designed and implemented by the Powers That Be to keep everybody off-kilter, angry at each other, victimized, and totally distracted from what's really going on.

This is no excuse. And yet, at the same time, it's the truth: Everybody on this planet has been suppressed, oppressed, attacked and victimized at some point. **All human beings, not just people of color, are ENSLAVED in a system that uses us all as pawns, sucking us dry.**

The only way out of this is for everybody to see the game and stop playing. The only way out of this is for people to come together and realize the truth—all lives matter.

Because they do.

Occult aside

If you believe in reincarnation and if you believe we've all incarnated as humans on this planet (and no doubt other planets) for millions of years or more, it just stands to reason every one of us has been every color of the rainbow and every sex imaginable over and over again. It also stands to reason that every single one of us has been on the receiving end of torture, abuse, discrimination, prejudice and every other possible kind of horror, thousands of times over.

Nobody has escaped abuse. Unfortunately, the way the matrix has been rigged, we don't remember those past experiences. We're stripped at the "light"—most often which is actually not the "Light of God" it's made out to be, but rather a false light projection that is technologically designed to remove all memory from the soul/spirit at "death," and then spit that soul/spirit back into the matrix to do it all over again.

Ever wonder why you don't have past life recall? This is why.

It's a huge complicated (occult) story that's not appropriate to get into here. If you're interested in the details, check out *Cracking the Matrix.* But the short version is, there's "light" (IE. the white light of the visible light spectrum) and then there's love. In the matrix, the former is designed to mimic the latter and keep us trapped in the matrix. The key here is people learning *discernment* so they can tell the truth from the false light—and choose accordingly

Which is what I'm trying to do with this book. I'm trying to expose the lies around "sexuality" that keep us blind and enmeshed in the matrix so we can gain discernment and set ourselves free.

And if you believe in karma? Well, that's just a program that seals the deal, guaranteeing you'll be spit back into the most painful life possible next time around.

I remember working in Indian Country, one Native editor I knew mentioned that she had been told by a Native shaman that Native Americans were the reincarnated race of white Atlanteans who had slaughtered and enslaved the brown-skinned people of Lemuria for thousands of years. That coming back and being conquered and subjugated by the whites from Europe was their karma.

True? Who knows?

Again, my point, is: When are we going to start seeing through the web of deceit and stop serving ourselves up to the real abusers and controllers? When are we all going to wise up, get along, and take care of each other?

Chapter 12

Why It's So Hard to See What's Happening

Ever since I wrote *Cracking the Matrix,* I've been asked time and again on podcasts and radio shows, "If there really is a global agenda to subjugate humanity, why haven't we seen it? Why isn't it obvious?"

Each time I get asked, I'm tempted to blurt something like, "How much more obvious must it get?" But I control myself. Because I know that as weird as things are getting, billions of people still perceive the current global situation as just "the way life is."

We've been conditioned for so long via so many routes—education, history, politics, media, religion, and entertainment—to think so little of ourselves, we don't expect anything other than what we've got. The image of human beings as fundamentally flawed creations, corrupt in mind and body and easily led astray, is indelibly stamped in our brains.

As a result, we believe constant conflict, mayhem, wars, corruption, confusion and disaster are no more than our due—the natural result of human nature.

The first and greatest lie

I've said it before and no doubt will say it again: Humanity is innately good-hearted and compassionate. For heaven's sake, in 2019, self-help book sales in the US increased by 13 percent, with over 40 million books being sold.[12] Globally, self-improvement books and courses represent an annual market worth $11 billion.

There are around six billion religiously-affiliated adults and children around the globe. Approximately three quarters of the world's population believes in a higher divine state of existence and consciously strives to attain or align with it.[13]

So much for the idea that humanity is simply a hotbed of nasty.

Everywhere I've gone around the world—in first, second and third-world countries—I've only met decent, loving, generous people. Granted, the poorer the country, the more obvious the happiness and generosity are. (Which should tell us something right there.) The vast majority of humanity just wants to get along and overall feel like they're valuable and contributing something to the world.

Are there degenerates, psychopaths, sociopaths, murderers, rapists, and thieves in the world? Of course. Are they in the majority like we're being led to believe? No That's another lie designed to make us remain in a state of fear and near-PTSD at all times—a state that removes us from common sense and rational thinking, making us malleable, controllable and suggestible, begging for global authoritarian leaders to save us from ourselves and take over.

Blatant exposure

I have heard through the grapevine that part of the White Hat / Black Hat "Rules of Engagement," as it were, involves open disclosure by the Black Hats of their overall malicious intentions. This, of course, is directly attributable to satanic protocol which requires the same.

Because if victims are fully informed of what's about to be perpetrated upon them and they do nothing about it, they remove themselves from victim status and become complicit. In other words:

Informed inaction = agreement

Everything the Black Hats have planned for us is publicly available information. For example, the Event 201 pandemic tabletop exercise held October 18, 2019 in New York, hosted by The Johns Hopkins Center for Health Security in partnership with the World Economic Forum and the Bill & Melinda Gates Foundation, spelled out the COVID scenario in detail, exactly as it went down the following year.[14]

All the Word Economic Forum summits in Davos, Switzerland are recorded and the recordings and transcripts are public domain. In these summits, humans are referred to as "hackable animals,"[15] AI is coolly presented as the solution to all our problems, ESG scores and 15-minute SMART cities are touted as answers to global problems, digital currencies are promoted, as well as plans for taking meat and dairy off peoples' tables and replacing them with insects, etc. etc. All these agendas are openly discussed.

And what does the world's population do with the information? Nothing.

Movies like *Wag the Dog* clearly show how easily public

perceptions are being manipulated by the media. Movies like *1984, The Matrix, Terminator* (et al), *Total Recall, Elysium, Gattaca* and dozens of others, clearly spell out humanity's dystopian future if we do nothing.

And we do nothing.

Why?

Because—aside from being hypnotized by corporate-owned mainstream media into thinking everything is fine and that it's simply business as usual in our dysfunctional world—normal, decent human beings literally can't fathom that something so fundamentally wrong, plans so blatantly evil, would ever be carried out. We think, "No one in their right mind would or could do such horrible things to us."

See how our compassionate, loving human nature is being used against us?

The trivialization game

Another reason we don't see what's going on is because we're too sophisticated to believe in such a thing as evil. We believe in the scientific method. We worship logic and depend upon physical evidence for things. (Available WEF videos and testimonies not withstanding.)

For those who still believe in things like God and evil, the situation isn't much better because Western religion trivializes evil. The basic story posited by Christianity is "The devil is amongst us (a big guy with red skin, horns and hooves), and he's trying to get us to do bad things. Turn away from the devil and accept Jesus into your heart and become good and go to heaven."

Presenting the devil as a ridiculous, singular entity that any sane, logical person would laugh at and dismiss pretty much guarantees we dismiss the whole concept. And if we do buy into the idea that this scary dude exists, the solution is Jesus. So, no worries mate!

Either way we don't consider other possibilities and we don't ask any questions.

The other way Western religion keeps the evil afoot on this planet hidden from view is by diminishing evil through association with a ton of ideas about sin.

People who have sex before marriage are called sinful. Men who kick a dog are called evil. Women who prostitute themselves for money are called evil. This trivialization of evil inoculates us against the true meaning of the word. So when real evil shows up—the satanic ritual rape of babies and young children, torture, cannibalism, sex trafficking—we barely notice.

The love of money is declared evil and then the Church demands economic support for golden miters, chalices, elaborate crowns, purple satin robes and sumptuous palaces for their priests to dwell in.

I don't want to demean people's beliefs, but taken at face value, religions present such a stream of easily-dismissed nonsense and hypocrisy that by sheer association rational people end up inoculated against any and all talk about evil, the devil, and satanic forces. Which means by default, the reality of a negative interdimensional intelligence lurking on this planet with humanity's enslavement on its mind goes unseen.

Once we think we know what's what—once we believe that evil isn't real, that rich elite humans wouldn't sell out their entire planet for personal gain, that Jesus will save us, etc.—we stop asking questions. We stop looking for other explanations beyond our own culpability for why life on Earth is such a crap deal and why conditions just seem to be getting worse and worse despite all our best efforts to the contrary. (And all those self-help books!)

No questions = invisibility

Spiritual culpability

Spirituality doesn't come off any better. Sixty years into the New Age Movement, everybody is so fixated on "the Light" and the chronic need to have "happy positive thoughts" all the time, nobody in the spiritual arena has the energy or the inclination to examine the dark side.

Contemplating evil doings is considered "fear-based thinking." Worse, if you spend time allowing such fear-based thoughts and ideas into your head (ideas like I'm promoting here), as a creative manifesting being, you'll inevitably draw bad things down upon your head. Your reality will degrade and you'll end up in a place you don't want to be. So, for God's sake, don't look at any bad stuff. Just keep searching for the Light. (Never mind it's already inside us!)

This is, of course, classic spiritual bypassing. But oh! What a convenient spiritual philosophy to promote so people don't look in dark corners and question what's going on around them. Is it humanly possible to manifest an amazing, liberated life while being unconsciously manipulated by anti-life intelligences and global elites who don't have your best interests at heart?

Is it possible to thrive and prosper while blindly following duplicitous agendas designed to bring you harm, curtail your freedom and limit your choices in life?

I don't think so.

Trained to obedience

I hardly need to mention this, but one more reason so many remain so blind is human beings have been trained to be obedient since time immemorial. Be obedient to God so you won't go to hell. Be obedient to your overlord so you won't get beaten to death or starve. Be obedient to your teacher so you won't flunk out of school and have to work at a blue-collar job for the rest of your life. Be obedient to your military leader so you won't get court-martialed and shot. Be obedient to your father, your mother, your pastor, your local police authorities, FEMA, the WEF, the CDC, the WHO.

Whatever. Whoever. The message for thousands of years has been the same: Don't step out of line. Do not question authority or the accepted narrative. Or else.

We are programmed into this. But there is also the whole "I want to be a good little girl or boy" impulse that's innately part of our human psyche. We naturally want to get along. We naturally want to be good. Not just to please authorities. But because we inherently want to please others out of our pure good nature.

Poor humanity! Is there even a chance we can wake up in time? Yes!

Good odds

Once upon a time I interviewed Dr. John Hagelin, a renowned quantum physicist who conducted pioneering research at CERN (the European Center for Particle Physics) and at the Stanford Linear Accelerator Center, developing a highly successful grand unified field theory based on the superstring. He is also well-versed in consciousness studies and meditation, and is currently serving as the president of Maharishi International University in Fairfield, Iowa.

To the best of my ability to recall, essentially our conversation went something like this:

ME: "Dr. Hagelin, do you believe if enough people wake up to what's going on, the energetic "field effect" of their higher consciousness could positively affect and uplift the whole of humanity?"

HAGELIN: "Yes, I do."

ME: "So, do you have any idea how many people on this planet have to wake up before the effects in consciousness are great enough that the whole planet can shift into a more enlightened state of awareness?"

HAGELIN: "Actually, yes. I've calculated it will take approximately one tenth of one percent of the world's population to make such a shift possible."

One tenth of one percent! I'm not much at math, but unless I'm mistaken, with the current global population around eight billion, that means we need at least eight million people waking up, firing up the torch of truth to light the pathway for others to find their way to freedom and the New World we dream of and yearn to create.

Eight million people? Surely, we have that in the bag—and then some!

EXPLORATION

Conspiracies are as old and normal as civilization itself. Let me ask you, have you ever hung out with a bunch of friends and bought cigarettes illegally? Booze? Pot? Something harder? Congratulations. You've officially been part of a conspiracy, which is defined by Merriam-Webster as: "An agreement to perform together an illegal, wrongful, or subversive action."

Anybody who pays their tax accountant to cook the books is part of a conspiracy. Anybody who has an affair on their husband or wife is part of a conspiracy. Conspiracies are a dime a dozen, constantly playing out in the bedroom and the boardroom, in the Senate and on the stage. Factions—whether political, economic, educational, scientific, religious or individual—are always trying to secretly one up and control other factions.

The key word here being "secretly."

Of course, the bigger the agenda and the more people involved, the greater the vulnerability and thus the less likely absolute secrecy can be maintained. Which means that smear tactics and disinformation programs must be frequently and effectively deployed. Is it surprising that secret organizations running the Elites' global agenda might use media programming to subvert public knowledge of their actions? Is it surprising that "educated people" might be trained to have a negative knee-jerk reaction to the "C" word?

Doesn't it make good sense to set those kinds of defense mechanisms up?

Once upon a time, I was one of those well-educated, well-trained knee-jerk sceptics. If anybody had told me (which someone eventually did) about the existence of a secret elite cabal with global mischief on its mind, I would have laughed in their face. (Which I did.) But then one thing led to another and I ended up reading the 500-page, highly annotated book *The Unseen Hand: An Introduction to the Conspiratorial View of History* by Ralph Epperson.

That one book, published in 1985, was so well researched and comprehensive that it effectively destroyed my sense of normal reality, obliterating the rock-solid American Republican View bequeathed to me by my family. I then went on to read other books that imploded my economic and social understanding, including *The Creature from Jekyll Island: A Second Look at the Federal Reserve.* (The current 2010 reprint is #2 in economic policy and development and #3 in money and monetary policy on Amazon.)

Back in the 1980s, my conspiratorial knowledge was limited to economics, and I tried to share what I was learning with my WASP family living in one of the wealthiest areas of America outside Washington D.C. Yeah, right. *That* wasn't happening. I tried to share information with my professional friends in network television. (You'd think people in communications would be interested in learning about stuff to communicate. But nope.) And my spiritual friends couldn't have cared less about the history of the central banking system either.

Graciously I was informed that information contrary to the status quo and mainstream media messaging was a "conspiracy" and that conspiracies were for fruit cakes. Friends forgave my gullibility, chalking it up to a temporary glitch in my operating system. My parents—well, my parents had yet to forgive me for voting Democratic. God knows what they thought about my rants about the Rockefeller and Rothchild empires.

Never mind the large amount of openly-available proof. Forget the fact that every mainstream magazine in America has, at one time or another, published in-depth articles about secret societies and their not-so-secret agendas. (Or at least the agendas the secret societies wished to have known.) Everybody I knew was part of the "impossible" crowd.

"An economic conspiracy is impossible to prove," people said. And when I handed them a book saying, "Here's the proof. Check the documentation between pages 272 to 312," they refused to look at the information because it was "obviously incorrect," so why bother checking it out?

If they actually looked at it, then where would they be? In the same fruitcake boat as me. And that was unacceptable. Best to resort to scornful ridicule followed by a conciliatory invitation to have drinks somewhere and move on with both status quo and personal comfort zones safely intact.

Other common feedback lines were: "People just aren't

smart enough to perpetrate the kinds of things you're talking about." Or "Humans just aren't patient enough to plot for thousands of years to gain control of the world." Or "It's absolutely impossible to keep something like a global agenda for totalitarian economic control a secret."

The other excuse people used was, "I know what's going on. I keep abreast of the news. I read *The New York Times* and *The Washington Post*. If something like this were happening, I'd know about it. I'd see the signs."

Sigh. The signs are all around us. We just don't see them.

Inattentional blindness

The average human brain receives approximately 11-million bits of information per second about the world around it. Because we literally can't handle that amount of input without going insane, a sensory gating system installs itself early on in our baby brain's development, filtering that enormous amount of data down to an average of 60 bits per second.

Sixty bits per second. That's all it takes for a human being to get a college degree, have a conversation or fly the space shuttle. Obviously, with an intact sensory gating system, seeing the Big Picture is a difficult task.

Then there's the odd way the human brain deals with what little data does make it into conscious awareness. Human beings perceive, and thus think, in terms of duality.

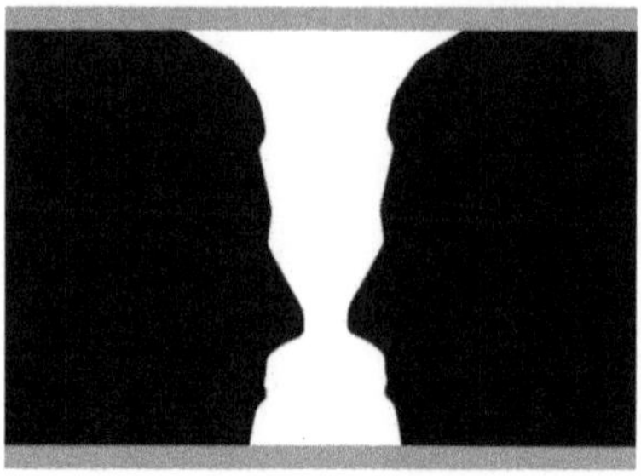

We perceptually function in terms of differences and either/or. It's how our brains are wired to discern reality. And a figure-ground study created in 1915 by Danish psychologist Edgar Rubin called the Rubins-vase shows what I mean.

It's easy to see the white vase. Right? But then the image of two men facing each other shows up. But then it switches back to the white vase. Back and forth. Either/or. It's almost impossible to hold the two images at the same time.

But this dualistic visual filter isn't the only thing coloring and even obscuring reality. I know, for an absolute fact, that it's not just deeply-guarded, subversive plots that we miss. People miss the most blatantly obvious, in-your-face things everyday. Let me tell you how I discovered this.

I was sitting in a room with 62 other people when Marilyn Schlitz, Ph.D., researcher, social anthropologist and senior scientist at the California Pacific Medical Center, gave a talk on something called inattentional blindness and selective attention.

During the talk she played a video of six people in a large office hallway rapidly passing a volleyball around the group. Three people wore white shirts and three people wore black shirts. All of us attending the lecture were instructed to count the number of times the ball was passed between the people wearing the white shirts.

About 20 seconds into the video, I lost count and gave up

the exercise. To my amazement, a big guy in a gorilla suit suddenly materialized out of nowhere, standing in front of the circle of people passing the ball. He faced the camera, beat his chest, then turned and walked off while the ball exercise was still in motion.

"How many of you saw something unusual in this video?" Schlitz asked a minute later when the clip finished. One other woman and I raised our hands. The 61 other people saw nothing out of the ordinary. When she ran the same video again, telling us to simply watch the video and not count ball passes, there the gorilla was, clear as day to everyone.

Audience reactions ranged from stunned to indignant to outraged. A couple people accused Schlitz of playing two different videos to trick them. But who needs somebody to trick us when we already trick ourselves? The whole point of the exercise was to show people how much information humans constantly miss—ENORMOUS things like a freaking GORILLA standing directly in front of a camera in a small hallway.

Which begs the question: If I can miss seeing a six-foot gorilla standing the equivalent of ten feet away in plain sight, what else am I not seeing?

Chapter 13

Moving Mountains

Learning how to stay passionate, creative, and calmly optimistic in an insane world is not easy. But that's the job at hand for all of us as we move forward during these strange and deeply significant times.

It's up to us to dream and set forward a future where life is honored and respected. Into a future where all beings are allowed to live in peace. Where prosperity and health aren't costly transactional operations. Into a future where children exuberantly explore and freely express themselves in expansive, unprogrammed ways.

To get to that future we have to be capable of not only dreaming it, but actualizing it. And to be capable of actualizing it we have to be potent and present. And potency, as I've discovered, requires being deeply embodied and grounded to the earth—precisely the empowered orientation that a couple thousand years of religious and cultural programming have been designed to guide us away from.

Scriptural deceit

Those of us raised in one of the three Abrahamic religions of Islam, Judaism and Christianity have been taught that we are the dust of the Earth and basically nothing. Because "nothing" and "dust" were considered equivalent. Dry. Dead. Worthless This teaching, like so many religious and spiritual teachings around the world, is a deliberate twisting of the truth. Yes, my body and the body of Earth are of one substance. But as we have seen over and over, that "substance," including dust, is purely energetic.

E=MC2

It's all the same thing. A massive, incomprehensible, infinite, evolving, intelligent force capable of building and creating mountains and oceans and universes. Being deeply embodied and grounded to the earth is the most fantastically potent state. It's where all that we are integrates and real power resides. Not in political parties. Not in money. Not in science. Not in atom bombs. Not in AI. But in our energetic selves.

Aligned with telluric forces, life/love explodes through us in a mating dance—a creative process that ensures there is nothing else possible in the future for us but more life, more love, more intimate expansive connection and ever greater possibilities.

Aligning with our Earth Mother is aligning with the true north of our own being. When we go beyond the *concept* of such a possibility and embody the living waters of spirit which are also the living waters of earth, we step into our authority. We step into the consciousness Jesus referred to where: "If ye have faith as a grain of mustard seed, ye shall say unto this mountain, 'Remove hence to yonder place;' and it shall remove; and nothing shall be impossible unto you."[16]

Of course, this kind of power seems pretty far-fetched to people whose inner authority has been adroitly hijacked, who rely on truth from the mainstream media, politicians and duplicitous agencies like the CDC, WHO and WEF, who run to the nearest drugstore to get the latest flu shot at the first sneeze, who haven't walked barefoot upon the earth or sat quietly under a tree (without a phone!) for decades.

Maybe Jesus could move mountains. Or Superman. But lil' ol' me?

It's up to us

Obviously, the "you" that can literally move mountains isn't the personal "you"—the ego personality with all its issues and triggers, fears and phobias, biases and unconscious programming running around in a delusional social matrix set in place by interdimensional forces and their global elitist lackeys.

It isn't the "you" that thinks about power in any personal way at all.

The "you" that can move mountains is the spirit you that yearns for world peace. It's the spirit you that yearns for kindness—for yourself and all others. It's the spirit you that knows that life—all life— deserves respect and equal consideration. It's the spirit you that yearns for an end to violence and all the suffering on this planet by any living creature.

It's the spirit you that refuses to seek vengeance as you cradle the shattered body of your dead son or daughter in your arms, looking the very enemy who took that life in the eye, filled with rage, consumed beyond all understanding by grief ... the you who, despite the volcanic rage and agony says, "NO! I will not perpetuate the violence that took my child. The cycle of revenge and killing stops here, with me, NOW! This is how I honor his life. Her life. Not with more death and killing ... but with more life."

THAT is the love, the power that moves mountains.

That is the love, the power, that births new realities. That is the love and the power that dreams a better future and actualizes it. Because that is the love and the power of life itself moving through us, as us.

Lean on the body

I have been taught—we all have been taught—to count on the mind. To figure things out logically. But the mind is so easily tricked! It's actually the last thing we can reliably depend upon during dangerous times.

The body, on the other hand, is a grand truth-meter.

Unlike the mind, the body never lies. It always tells us the truth of what's *really* going on, both within and without. The heart, the gut, know what's what before the mind has a clue. And that's because the body—the heart, the gut—are connected with the river of life, aligned with its flow.

Studies have shown that the gut and heart know the answers before the brain does. In an emergency, the gut and the heart are already propelling the body to safety before the brain has a clue. Body wisdom is nature's wisdom and unfathomably intelligent.

Which brings me around to the subject of trust.

Faith versus trust

The word "trust" is believed to derive from the Old Norse word "traust," meaning "help, confidence, protection, support." But there are questions about that. The most reliable origin is the proto-Indo-European world "deru" — to be "firm, steadfast, hard, solid." By the time "trust" came into common usage in the West around 1200 AD, it meant: "reliance on the veracity, integrity, or other virtues of someone or something; religious faith."

Jesus used the word "faith" in that scriptural quote two thousand years ago when the meaning behind the word was close to its root "deru."

What he was really saying is, if we have the firmness, the steadfast confidence of a mustard seed—an apparently inanimate object which, by nature of its awareness of its true energetic essence and inevitable life as a live, growing being—we can prevail over anything. (BTW, studies show that plants have consciousness, feel pain, and clearly communicate with one another.[17])

The steadfastness he refers to isn't a matter of having faith, as in the later definition which places our reliance on the veracity, integrity, or other virtues of someone or something outside us. He's talking about the strength that comes from the certainty of self-knowledge.

Awareness of self as an infinite, eternal spirit of pure love.

"Trust is listening deeply to your own being," says Jacqueline Hobbs, better known as Oracle Girl. And I couldn't have said it better myself. Unfortunately, the way society has been programmed—the way *we* have been programmed—the LAST person we listen to and trust is ourselves. We have been rigorously schooled to always look outside ourselves for answers and direction—from teachers and gurus, politicians and economists, scientists and doctors, religious leaders and priests, and now, the Lord God Google.

This programming has been deliberate. When the chips are down, the Powers That Be want everyone looking to *them*—depending upon *their* messages, *their* answers, *their* rules—for global salvation.

So, how do we develop trust in ourselves?

Back to the body

Pretty much everything in the matrix is inverted. (Like the pentagram.) After decades being trained by gurus and instructed by self-help books to focus on the "light" and to get up and out of my body and go somewhere out in space, away from Earth where bliss and freedom reside, coming to the realization that my body is my safe place has been a shock.

Coming to the realization that the answer to my fears and worries, insecurities and uncertainties is diving down and into my body—consciously resting in the sensed power of embodied love/life—has proven difficult to accept with my mind. I mean, if I'm spirit, shouldn't I be focused on spiritual things?

Yes, well, what is the body really? You know the answer by now. The body and spirit are one. And when I practice resting consciously in my body, I can feel the love. It's so real! So palpable!

And as I get more and more in touch with that feeling of love and the enormous, unstoppable grace and power of pure being, feeling the power that flows through me, that is me, that is not "human"—a power that is energetic, ineffable, and creative beyond measure—over time, that practiced experience builds trust. I am then filled with the knowingness that this is safe haven indeed. I can't put my finger on it. But I begin to trust the reality of this power more than any thing I could ever touch.

Distractions

Is getting to this place easy? For some, yes. For others, not so much. It's totally individual. Remember, you weren't raised in a Tibetan monastery and taught to meditate hours and hours every day by yourself. Raised in the US, like me, you were trained to focus on externals.

In the West, we are relentlessly bombarded with sensory information screaming for our attention. A hundred different kinds of potato chips packaged in neon plastic compete for our eyes and dollars and taste buds. Video games—most of which are violent, filled with gore, and highly sexual—suck the life force and attention of 97 percent of US boys and 83 percent of US girls for hours every day.[18] TV, movies, YouTube, take up more time fixated outwardly on a screen, brain entrained into a malleable alpha state, soaking up the messages.

And then there are cell phones.

Cellphone users in the US look at their phones 144 times a day, spending an average of four hours and 25 minutes on their phones—a figure that's up 52 percent from 2022.[19] Millennials spend even more time on their phones, an average 5.7 hours a day. That's 2,081 hours a year. In ten years, that's 20,811 hours. Which is 2.4 years spent looking at memes, texts, Instagram, Snapchat, Twitter, Reddit etc. etc.

Seriously? Years spent sucked into a tiny phosphorescent screen filled with ... what? Certainly not information telling you that you are the most powerful, incandescently beautiful, tender, creative, generous, kind, loving spirit on the entire planet. Nope. Anything and everything BUT that.

It's probably like asking you to pluck out an eyeball or cut off a limb, but the less time you spend on such trivial devices and the more you time you can dedicate to getting in touch with life, nature, your body, your feelings, and your intuition, the better.

Heaven

Jesus is credited with saying something else: "God's kingdom is within you."[20] This is often translated as "The kingdom of heaven lies within." But what did he mean by "God's kingdom" and "heaven" anyway? Did he mean bliss? Peace? Eternal life? Rainbows and unicorns with harps on clouds forever?

Frankly, at this point in the game, if I had to choose one word as a definition for "heaven," I think it would be "certainty."

If I can be certain, it means I am "deru" —to be "firm, steadfast, hard, solid" in any given situation. And by certainty I'm not talking about facts and figures and statistics. I'm not talking about concepts and beliefs. All those things can be changed and manipulated to mean any number of things. Which is why, when we get caught up in the mind and the world of factoids, things can get so confusing.

No, what I'm talking about is the *inner certainty of the body and its intelligence*. For example, ever just "known" something? That somebody was going to walk in the room? Or you needed to turn right even though Siri was telling you to turn left? Or you just "knew" not to trust somebody you met—and six weeks later you find out s/he stole all your best friend's money?

Inner knowing—that's certainty.

If I can be certain and always know which way to go and what to choose no matter what the hell is happening, I will have "traust," meaning "help, confidence, protection, support" from *myself*. And if I have trust ... total trust ... (imagine having total, absolute, complete, trust in yourself and life! Imagine it!) Wouldn't that be blissful? Peaceful? Heavenly?

Yeah, I think so too.

EXPLORATION

Something that really helps with this getting-in-the-body-and-in-touch-with-life's intelligence process is something called "somatic tracking." You can find dozens of somatic exercises on the web, and I highly recommend checking them out. But one of the simplest things you can do is set aside 15 minutes, set aside your phone (like turn it off), and simply sit with your bare feet on the floor (or on the ground outside), get comfortable, and get in touch with your body.

Starting at your feet, simply notice how every inch of your body feels—feet, ankles, calves, knees, thighs ... and on up, step-by-step, body part by body part.

Breathe calmly and normally as you do this, noticing feelings, sensations, energy, colors, movement, stagnation ... whatever shows up. The slower you go and the longer you take becoming deeply aware of your entire body and your feelings, the more in-tune, grounded, and relaxed you'll feel.

This practice will help you develop acute sensitivity and receptivity to the promptings of intuition and the inner guidance of life/love. And that alignment will always take you safely towards more life and more love.

Chapter 14

River Crossings

River crossings are tricky. Rushing, turbulent waters, slippery rocks, no visible footing, no hand rail, no assurance you'll make it to the other side. River crossings are also symbolic.

Back in my early spirituality days, I read a book called *Brother of the Third Degree* written by Will Garver in 1894 at the height of the Golden Age of Occultism. In it, the young hero, Alphonso Colono, sails from his home in Mexico to Paris to undergo various initiations at the hands of the Illuminati. (IE. the White Brotherhood). Among other tests, in a thrilling moment of self-abnegation, he agrees to a non-sexual, "pure" marriage with his beloved soulmate Iole.

At the time, I was greatly uplifted by Alphonso's high-minded sexual sacrifice. Now, with so many veils of spiritual programming ripped from my eyes, I look back on that part of the book and think, "What a load of baloney designed to keep the main characters frustrated and miserable!"

I now wonder who Will Garver really was. And what was his agenda? Was he duped and ignorant of the gross sexual propaganda he was spreading? Or was he privy to The Lie that sex is base and lowly and part of disseminating that lie? I guess it doesn't matter now. But I do wonder!

Anyway, back to river crossings.

At the end, Alphonso takes his final test. He lies in the bottom of a canoe with no oars, hands folded serenely across his breast, and is cast off one side of a wide river with a thundering waterfall just downstream. By faith in a Higher Power alone, he guides the canoe safely to the opposite shore where angels, as well as Iole and gathered members of the White Brotherhood, proudly await.

I was reminded of that story this morning as I lay in bed in the early dawn's light, thinking about the world we live in today and the perilous river crossing we face, with mandates, economic collapse, cyber attacks, nuclear war, the Great Reset, bioweapons, pandemics, AI, and whatever else the global elites have in store for us in these last days of negative control.

Instead of getting upset about what might or might not be waiting for us downstream, I let the vision of total world domination fade away. Yes, we are currently experiencing a rapid slide into totalitarianism, mind control, social fragmentation, and general demoralization. It's the Last Days of Pompeii, the Fall of Rome, the Sinking of Atlantis and Armageddon all rolled into one.

Humanity appears to be trapped within a single fragile canoe, racing downstream towards the Waterfall of Doom with no paddles, no motor, and no possibility of hope in sight.

Not true.

That's just the propaganda message being pushed at us day and night.

Don't listen to it.

The Great Awakening

A great yearning for a new experience—a happy and healthy life on Earth—has arisen in humanity. We ache to throw off the chains and shackles that have dragged us down for so long. And yet to have this new experience, we must first and foremost finally see what's really going on. And when we finally see what's really going on, we realize there's no fixing what was designed to break in the first place.

Our current social structures cannot get us to the future we desire because they were designed to take us where we don't want to go ... into the abyss of division and despair where we let go all desire for personal liberty and sovereignty and welcome complete external control as our only salvation.

Once you see this, things get simple really fast.

We are spirit beings of pure love. Nature is our nature. Once we turn our attention away from the sorrowful, death-laden present and embrace Who We Really Are, a door to a whole new reality opens before us. And the "Open Sesame" for that door are a couple simple questions:

"What does my heart say? What does my soul yearn for?"

Loving companionship that is mutually supportive. Community. A healthy planet. Free thinking. The open development of inventions and markets for creating healthy foods, healthy minds, healthy bodies and a stable environment. An expansive educational system for children that opens up their minds, encourages their unique abilities and invites them to blossom. A localized, non-intrusive system of governing that strives to support everyone's individual freedom while still supporting the whole.

Isn't this what most of us dream of? What does your heart

say? What does your soul yearn for? Peace, if it's to be birthed for real, has to happen within each and every one of us. And then we need to take physical steps to make those dreams manifest.

Perhaps you feel called to start a local school with a creative curriculum for children. Or you feel the urge to start a neighborhood garden. Or invent something. Or make music. Or maybe get involved in local politics. Maybe you feel the urge to move to the country—or another state or town. If you feel the need to move, then move.

There is more than enough land and our world is still brimming with sufficient resources to support everyone once we get past the petty agendas we were trained to believe are important enough to kill and die for. Opportunities are here for all. Amazing discoveries and creations are waiting to be made once we see through and then abandon the taskmasters with their cruelty and greed, cold indifferent agendas and Not-So-Great Reset.

A new world is waiting for us—the one we pray and yearn for—when we come together despite everything, to create peace and take the responsibility for building it.

And what about all the people still trapped in the matrix? What about all the people still desperately trying to fix the old programs? Billions of people of good heart and intention struggling to find solutions in a system gone mad, bent on ripping the beating heart from its own chest?

Perhaps some will notice your life-oriented choices. Perhaps some will be drawn to your heart flame's signal and the scales will drop from their eyes. Perhaps you will say something, or simply reach out a helping hand, and that will finally inspire an "aha!"

Whatever your intuition urges you to do ... follow the prompt.

It sounds simple, and it is. But don't let simple fool you. Simplicity is always an indicator of truth. It's aligned with that whole topic of purity that was discussed in Chapter Four. Simply following your heart will always take you and your loved ones where you want to go.

Much love and aloha ~

Cate

ENDNOTES

1 *Candace Pert, Ph.D., Molecules of Emotion, Scribner; 1st edition* (*May* 8, 2010)

2 *Hosea 4:5*

3 *https://metro.co.uk/2023/10/16/forget-the-morning-coffee-have-an-orgasm-to-boost-productivity-19669114/?ico=trending-post-strip_item_3*

4 *https://isha.sadhguru.org/us/en/wisdom/video/having-multiple-partners-what-is-the-problem*

5 *https://www.pewresearch.org/internet/2008/09/16/teens-video-games-and-civics/*

6 *https://www.center4research.org/violent-video-games-can-increase-aggression/*

7 *https://www.therecoveryvillage.com/mental-health/gender-dysphoria/gender-dysphoria-statistics/*

8 *https://www.reuters.com/investigates/special-report/usa-transyouth-data/*

9 https://articles.mercola.com/sites/articles/archive/2023/10/15/protect-your-child-from-transgender-
10 https://dailycaller.com/2022/10/05/sex-change-industry-report-transgender-surgery-profit-cost/
11 https://blog.gitnux.com/self-help-industry-statistics/
12 https://www.pewresearch.org/religion/2012/12/18/global-religious-landscape-exec/
13 https://www.weforum.org/press/2019/10/live-simulation-exercise-to-prepare-public-and-private-leaders-______for- pandemic-response
14 https://youtu.be/hL9uk4hKyg4
15 https://www.britannica.com/science/infor mation-theory/Physiology
16 https://www.technologyreview.com/2009/08/25/210267/new-measure-of-human-brain-processing-speed/
17 Mathew 17:20 KJV
18 Communicative & Integrative Biology. 2021; 14(1): 176–185.
19 https://www.pewresearch.org/short-reads/2018/09/17/5-facts-about-americans-and-video-games/
20 https://www.consumeraffairs.com/cell_phones/cell-phone-statistics.html
21 Luke 17:20-21

Acknowledgments

The other day I got sucked into watching the romcom *A Family Affair* with Nicole Kidman playing an aging author who hooks up with her daughter's boss—a sexy and seemingly shallow actor locked into action hero roles. One line in the movie stood out, and it was when Nicole's character is at her publisher's offices, and the woman at some point asks her, "Why do you write?"

She replies, "Because it helps me know what I know."

That's very much been the case with me and this book. I never thought I'd write a book about sex and gender... but it's such a potent topic, and such a trigger for myself and so many others, I realized I needed to better understand sexual dynamics—seen and unseen—to accomplish my own healing.

Writing this has forced me to piece together so many different kinds of sexual and esoteric knowledge gathered from so many different times and places, starting with my own uncertain sexual "coming of age" and all the misinformation, uncertainty, and insecurity that came with it.

When COVID came long with all its totalitarian craziness. THAT woke me up and made me realize there was something I wasn't seeing—something I *wasn't meant to see.* Which led me to investigating the nature and presence of negative interdimensional influences on humanity, dragging us down. Which led to writing *Cracking the Matrix* . That investigation, plus my dive into the power of sexuality led directly to writing this book.

Now the information I put together has been passed on to you.

Discovering what you know

It's hard to know truth at the best of times. And in today's mad world, deep introspection and contemplation aren't exactly encouraged. Independent thinking outside the mainstream message is not valued. It's directly disapproved. The programming and distractions point us in every direction but *within.* And herd mentality sometimes seems the safest bet.

Becoming our best, wisest, most authentic selves requires independent thought and a willingness to explore ideas and conversations outside the norm. And then comes of the hard work of embodying and actualizing new truths when we learn them.

It's rare to find people who are brave enough to do this. So, instead of thanking my friends and my cats for putting up with me while I wrote all this, instead of thanking my editor and publisher (who for this project are non-existent!), I wanted to take the opportunity in the "acknowledgements" section to express my appreciation and admiration for *you,* dear reader.

Maybe this book wasn't such a stretch. Perhaps it was. Either way, hats off. I hope the information supports your continued growth on this spiritual/"physical" adventure here on Earth.

And if you have any questions or want to set up a conversation about all that's covered here, *and more,* please let me know. You can reach me at info@catemontana.com.

About the Author

A professional journalist specializing in alternative medicine, health, and consciousness, since her (surprise!) awakening in 2007, Cate has written five extremely different books: *Cracking the Matrix: 14 Keys to Individual & Global Freedom,* which takes a deep dive into the history, nature and impact of negative interdimensional forces on this planet; a feminist memoir, *Unearthing Venus: My Search for the Woman Within;* an explanation of the ego and enlightenment, *The E Word, Ego Enlightenment & Other Essentials*; and a spiritual novel, *Apollo & Me.* A champion for the unlimited human and freedom, she speaks about actualizing and embodying our full spirit nature united with Earth's intelligence as the antidote to the shadow forces currently keeping humanity from effective sacred activism and true change. She has a master's degree in psychology and lives in Hawaii.

Check out her weekly writings at **cmontana.substack.com** and her other books at catemontana.com

www.ingramcontent.com/pod-product-compliance
Lightning Source LLC
Chambersburg PA
CBHW051159120626
46547CB00012B/1121
9798991113908